Made In Bradford

Editor: M Y Alam

University of
Chester
Warrington Campus

route

First published by Route
PO Box 167, Pontefract, WF8 4WW
e-mail: info@route-online.com
web: www.route-online.com

ISBN: 978-1-901927-32-0
ISBN (10 Digit): 1 901927-32-6

Editor:
M Y Alam

Support:
Ian Daley, Isabel Galan

Cover Design
Andy Campbell
www.dreamingmethods.com

Printed by Bookmarque, Croydon

A catalogue for this book is available from the British Library

Route is an imprint of ID Publishing
www.id-publishing.com

This book was possible thanks to support from
Joseph Rowntree Foundation

Contents

Acknowledgements

From initial idea through to finished product, this book has relied on the talents, patience and support of many colleagues and friends. Despite the best efforts of all concerned, the realisation of this book has not always taken an easy or straightforward route. One of the more difficult things to deal with, I now find, is choosing the right words to acknowledge those who have played some part in its making. On such pages, you will usually see words which aim to convey gratitude, appreciation or acknowledgment. At the bare minimum, this is a necessary professional courtesy. In some cases, however, the practice of formal acknowledgment becomes a way of revealing the truer nature of the work; reliance on others is not only appreciated, it is vital.

First and foremost, I would like to especially thank those who lie at the heart of this book, the men who took part in the Joseph Rowntree Foundation research project, *British-Pakistani Men from Bradford: Linking Narratives to Policy*. They have been consistently generous, good-spirited and understanding. Social research of the kind that this book is based upon would be impossible without the participation of individuals who are prepared to allow near strangers into their lives for whatever duration. Gaining their trust and experiencing their honesty has been my privilege and no doubt, on occasion at least, their burden. Their time, trust, good humour, enthusiasm and insights have all combined to affirm the more positive facets of life, including the occasionally jading world of social research itself. I remain grateful, indebted and only hope that I have done justice to their views and voices which rightfully form the basis of this book. Acknowledging them by name would be truer to the politics and ethics of the research. However, as a means of protecting their identities and ensuring their rights to privacy, the majority have asked not to be named. This is a request I fully understand and respect.

This JRF project was partly inspired by the work of American broadcaster and journalist, Studs Terkel. In particular, his books, including *Working* (1975), illustrate the way in which it is possible to lay everyday lives and voices on paper, for a mass audience in need of insight and the capacity to identify.

From the Joseph Rowntree Foundation, the support and assistance offered by Chris Goulden and Bana Gora has been regular and in abundance. I am mindful and appreciative of the JRF's willingness and desire to commit to the project through extending its obligations and supporting this particular publication. Members of the Advisory Group including Les Back, Karen Chouhan, M G Khan and Ludi Simpson have, in their own ways, aimed to ensure this book was done for the right reasons and in the most appropriate manner. In particular, Claire Alexander's valuable and always welcome feedback has been a source of motivation and direction. I hope she, like the others, is not disappointed.

Thanks are in order to Elaine Goldsbrough for her transcribing expertise, to Yunas Samad for his helpful remarks and willingness to listen and offer advice. The enthusiasm shown and the support offered by both Tarik Hussain and Mohammed Sultan over the last three years at least have helped sustain my interest in research, writing and in putting this book together.

I am as ever grateful for the inputs made by Ian Daley of Route. Apart from his publishing expertise and attention to detail, his support, trust and faith in this book – from fuzzy concept to finished and arguably less fuzzy product – is a testament to his politics, ethics, professionalism and decency.

The impetus and motivation for this book comes, in the main, from my friend and colleague, Charlie Husband. Without his presence, it's fair to say much of my own understanding would be less refined, clear or even considered than it occasionally appears to be. His patience, knowledge, experience but most of all, his humanity forms a rare but precious combination few individuals, especially those in the world of academia, can ever hope to have. Without wishing to undermine the role of the men whose narratives you will read in the pages that follow, this book would not exist without Charlie's drive, direction and faith. In more ways than one, I remain in his debt.

Finally, I'm not only thankful, but am impressed by my family's ability to put up with my unsociable working days and nights and occasional absenteeism from various commitments, especially over the last three years.

M Y Alam, Bradford, October 2006

Made In Bradford

Introduction
M Y Alam

The contents of this book began life as interviews with Bradfordian men of Pakistani Muslim heritage. The men took part in a twenty-one month qualitative social research project, conducted in Bradford and funded by the Joseph Rowntree Foundation (JRF)[1]. The hope was to gain insights into how identities are experienced, shaped and function in everyday life. The project also shed light on the overlapping debates surrounding citizenship, integration, ethnicity, and how Islam is lived and perceived in a contemporary, northern British inner city.

Although the JRF project aimed to link real life with social policy, the nature of the report steered it to an important but limited academic readership. At the core of the research, however, lay a commitment to ensuring the participants' voices maintained an important position in the project. The notion of doing yet another research project where the participants or research subjects occupy a relatively passive role – where research is done to them – didn't seem particularly fitting or necessary. Instead, ways in which the men would become drivers of the research itself, certainly in terms of direction and scope, featured from the outset. Coupled with this was a desire to find a means whereby their voices could be heard without secondary analysis or interpretation. This book contains those voices. Interview transcripts have been edited, structured and are now offered as individual but linked aspects of an anthology with its own coherence, flow and pace.

In order to communicate the rationale underpinning this book, it's necessary to outline the context in which the stories were gathered and, at the same time, to plot a few points on the narrative of the city to which they speak. For quite some time Bradford has been represented and perceived as a venue of challenges and conflicts, especially in relation to ideas and issues connected with ethnic and religious diversity. Bradford has a long and varied history in which immigration has played a significant part. German, Irish, Jewish, Italian and Eastern European influences remain woven into the social fabric of the city to this day. However, the impact of mid-to-late twentieth century non-white immigration from the Caribbean and South Asia tends to define the current external perceptions of the city and also feeds into the internal dimensions of city management. The diversity of its population, in terms of class, ethnicity and age, along with an interesting and occasionally fraught historical narrative, may well lead to public perceptions or imaginings that have very little connection with reality. Like all cities, however, Bradford has its own sense of identity that is strongly connected with its people and past.

Bradford is a large and diverse place, a significant chunk is still rural, green and, in parts, wealthy. At the same time, some inner city areas are clearly in need of economic and structural regeneration. Other locales – including Bingley, Thornton and Wilsden, for example – are more affluent, comfortable and do not usually attract the attention of policymakers, news media and other interested parties keen to refine and add to the city's biography. West Bowling, Manningham, Girlington, parts of Keighley and other neighbourhoods are, by comparison, poor and have relatively high concentrations of people with Asian heritage and ethnicity. What is barely mentioned, however, is that the majority of neighbourhoods in and around Bradford are overwhelmingly white, a significant number of which are also less than wealthy. Segregation exists but is more closely linked with economic and class markers, as opposed to those associated with ethnicity. What is still called 'white flight' (white people moving out of poorer areas into more affluent ones) could be more accurately labelled 'middle-class flight'. Bradford is clearly not Harrogate, nor is it York or even Leeds. Whether or not this is a good or bad thing is neither here nor there. Bradford's identity is not tied to what the conventional wisdom requires to be the norm. At times parts of it are conflicted and challenged. Like a character in a novel, however, the city itself becomes a point of identification, empathy and fosters close and deep connections especially with those who know it.

The texts presented here are based on interviews conducted between early 2004 and late 2005. Although I did the fieldwork myself, I was fortunate to share and discuss progress with my friend and co-researcher, Charlie Husband. Our initial motivation to conduct the research came during and soon after the 2001 disturbances – or riots, as they came to be known – in parts of northern England. The riots functioned as visible symptoms of a much deeper, but partly obscured, social and political reality. They were damaging in many ways and for many reasons. However, the way in which the events, the places and the people involved were represented and perceived, interested and provoked us beyond the usual expressions of concern. One aspect that stood out in our minds was that yet again, here was a group or type of individual being talked *about*, but not being talked *to*. Alongside this absence of real communication, a demonisation of this 'type', and indeed a wider ethnic group, was continuing to develop.

Post 9/11 and even more so after 7/7 – with the bombers hailing from nearby communities of Beeston and Dewsbury – Bradford's Muslims are increasingly associated with the 'War on Terror' and the apparently out-of-control rise in a more universal Islamic extremism. Meanwhile, a new direction has been pursued with regard to the perception and management of visible ethnic minorities in general. It turns out that multiculturalism, whether idea or policy, was at best misguided or at worst, wrong all along. Multiculturalism didn't help facilitate cultural integration because, the argument goes, it was said to have focused too much on ethnic diversity, as opposed to helping draw out or instil a mainstream kind of Britishness throughout the land. A consequence of multiculturalism, the wise and worthy are still at pains to tell us, is that even after more than fifty years (in some cases), some ethnic minorities are still ethnic minorities. The fact that many adhere to a different religious faith and are still attached to their country of origin, its culture and traditions, is deemed problematic because such attachments may mean a lesser propensity to identify with Britain and Britishness. By being so deeply 'ethnic', the new race logic flows, integrating into the British way of life is made less likely. In turn, this hinders access to the freedoms, opportunities and ambitions that Britain offers. More keenly, holding onto ethnic and religious identity is seen as a challenge, a problem and in some cases, a threat or at the very least, a risk to society at large.

The ongoing devaluation of multiculturalism has given rise to a more preferred mode and way of thinking that doesn't account for the ways in which imperialism continues to have an impact. Instead of multiculturalism as a means of at least acknowledging a historical legacy, 'community cohesion' is offered up as an antidote to symptoms which can be traced back to social divisions and inequalities. Although it's not entirely obvious as to what community cohesion actually means, what is true is that it's touted as a more realistic, practical and effective model. According to arguments being propelled by some, if Muslim women stopped wearing the veil, for example, a greater degree of integration and cohesion would be achieved. In this instance, the alienness of an ethnic culture as it is practiced is alleged to be the barrier to community cohesion, certainly not a lack of educational, economic and political infrastructure. Indeed, when such arguments are pursued, they are often done so in a way that suggests there is neither historical nor contemporary backdrop: British Muslim women are able to express their religious beliefs and practices precisely because they have a grounding within a British context, not because they are at odds with it.

As a result of changes in political ideology and policy, along with the resonance of global events, British Muslims today find themselves in the middle of interconnected debates touching on immigration, nationalism as well as citizenship and integration. The current fixation with integration in particular is skewed because it is invariably directed toward those ethnic minorities deemed severely problematic or at odds with what is often sold as a monolithic British way of life. This reasoning neglects to consider that while some may well be tied to an ethnic minority background or culture, they are also tied to what *they* perceive to be a British way of life. This may come as a newsflash to some, but being British and being Asian or Afro-Caribbean or Irish or Jewish or Muslim or Christian does not necessarily pose a dilemma or conflict.

The most recent origins of this new thinking can be partly traced back to the widely read, often cited and still oddly *un*controversial Ouseley Report which contains claims about how Bradford's communities are in themselves largely responsible for whichever social malaise happens to take the reader's (and writer's) fancy. In a city where fewer than a quarter of the population is of a black or minority ethnic background, Ouseley focuses on ethnicity as the principle marker of community, largely neglecting social class, income and even neighbourhood. As the stories presented here reveal, there's more to real life than a set of general and all-encompassing markers of identity that politicians, academics and, yes, even writers occasionally claim as truths.

In Britain, now more than ever, questions around loyalty and citizenship are regularly asked within a frame that juxtaposes Islam with Europe and, in so doing, frequently reassert the emergent tensions of having a Muslim presence in the West. Scrutiny and analysis has not only magnified, it has become more frequent. 7/7 and other high profile intelligence and policing episodes have in particular helped in maintaining the view that British Muslims, and

Islam, are a tangible threat to Britain's security and way of life. How the 'War on Terror' plays itself out is intricately connected to even the seemingly distant world of community cohesion, integration and citizenship. The argument being propelled aims to solidify the problem as one of immiscible ideologies or a clash of civilisations. The West and Islam are simply incompatible, we're asked to believe: a few drops of oil may well sit in the same vessel as a larger body of water, but it's just not in the nature of oil to 'mix' or integrate because it is of a fundamentally different molecule. As any chemistry student will know, however, under the right conditions, it is possible to mix, meld, fuse or otherwise integrate two distinct elements to come up with something new, different but still rooted in its original components.

British culture, like all cultures, is fluid and in a process of evolution. Britain's minorities, ethnic or otherwise, are part of a process that allows cultural crossover to take place; mainstream British culture now has more 'foreign' dishes on its menus than those that are purported to be indigenous, authentic or primordial British cuisine. Meanwhile, British Muslims find their own level of comfort by selecting and managing their own preferences: fashion, language, food, media, occupation, spirituality and politics are all subject to, at least in part, British values, sensibilities and even taste. Despite this under-reported reality, the rhetoric of some politicians, journalists and academics is built on the assumption that inside every Muslim there is the possibility of an enemy of the West waiting to get out, itching to make real his or her own piece of holy war. The way in which some Muslim communities (particularly working-class Pakistani and Bangladeshi), or even 'types' (young and male) are portrayed and perceived suggests that a construction of a pathologically alien, or at best insular and distinct culture is taking root. Now, more than ever, British Muslims are asked to prove themselves as not only loyal and peaceful, but also as integrated citizens.

Against this still developing and multilayered discussion, there is an absence of the normal, everyday voices of those who are usually talked about. Despite occasional news packages where young Muslims are given airtime, and in spite of programmes featuring arguably provocative and controversial viewpoints, there's a gap – a silence – that frustrates but doesn't actually surprise. This reality is a further factor which helped to shape our project, and in particular, this anthology. The voices in this book are as distinct to those belonging to the 'fundamentalists' of the 1990s or the 'extremists' of today and are more mainstream than those who appear to be integrated in all the right ways.

These stories are only borrowed for the purposes of this text and belong to a relatively small but varied group of everyday people who, like the rest of us, can talk about the everyday and the unusual in the same breath. Forced marriage, drugs and criminality, employment, racism, political representation, faith, freedom along with the notion of home and belonging were themes that recurred frequently during the interviews and are now reflected in the content of this book. Occasionally, the detail may seem mundane, other times profound and sometimes amusing. Whatever the nature of the content, insights that aren't usually accessible to the majority of us are present. What follows may function as alternatives, possibly even counter-narratives, to the prevailing direction of current debates. A greater validity and usefulness with a book of this nature, however, is that it rehumanises those who have been in various ways and at various historical moments, intentionally or not, dehumanised. Throughout, there remains an underlying vitality which may surprise some considering the range of experiences and events these men may face in their daily lives. In spite of dealing with and absorbing the less pleasant and more unwelcome aspects of life, their stories contain the most precious of human possessions: hope.

Bradford, like other inner cities, can be very much a fertile ground for researchers, journalists and writers in general. The way in which the city and some of its citizens have been represented, talked about and perceived, has at times been troubling because it appears to be stuck on a one-way traffic system where all the news is either bad or on its way to becoming so. Of course, like all cities, there are problems and challenges, the majority of which have very little to do with faith, ethnicity or the management of what are occasionally packaged as 'alien' cultures and groups. This book gives you a chance to see into a reality and experience which usually remains obscured – something authentic and real without interpretation or translation either by academic or reporter. Ultimately, you are, of course, free to make what you will of the pages to come. If you don't connect and communicate with the narrators, then the failing is not yours, certainly not down to the men whose time and patience I have taken, but is more likely due to my own shortcomings as researcher, editor and, at this point, writer.

[1] The JRF report (see back page for further details) contains a necessary academic interjection and discussion, not so much about the research data or what it does and does not suggest, but about the policy and political context to which the data relates, the nature of social research as well as ways in which part of Bradford's population and heritage have been already researched, analysed, and conceptualised.

Being British

Am I British? I've asked myself that enough times. Am I British? I think I am. When I was younger, teenage years, it was different. As you get older, you change. You grow for the better, you like to think. When you're younger, everything's a problem if you're a rebel. I used to be a rebel so I rebelled against everything, especially about being British. Being British? No way. But now it's different. I've been around a bit longer. Might have got a bit wiser.

One of the guys I work with, he's older than me, about early forties, I think. He doesn't consider himself British like I do. He was born here, too. When he was growing up, he had to take a lot of shit from white people – racism, fighting, aggro and all that. When I was growing up it was around as well, but so what? It's still around now, is all that. But him, he's still letting it get to him. He's not forgotten it – won't forget it. He's one of those type of people who can't forget some things. But myself, I think, 'Yeah, I am British. I must be British Pakistani or Pakistani British.' Whichever way you want to call it depends on you. Can't say there's nothing British about me, can I? If I think about it, most things about me are British.

I was born in Pakistan. Came here very young, with my mum, in seventy-three/seventy-four, too young to remember anything about it now. So, yeah, even though I was born back

25

in Pakistan, I didn't grow up knowing much about that place. I've been a few times but that's about it. I've noticed when I'm there that I'm not the same kind of Pakistani as people living in Pakistan. To them, in Pakistan, I'm British. A few people have told me about that; you go over there thinking it's your roots and all that and when you get there, they turn round and tell you to swivel on it, practically. For me it's not a problem any more. Like I said, what's wrong with admitting you're British or British Pakistani or British Asian? Some people, they're more proud of being Pakistani and being British doesn't come into it. They were born here and the only place and culture they've experienced is British but, admitting they're British, it's not something they want to do. I'm not a clever guy but I've a theory: admitting you're British makes you think of yourself as less Pakistani. Admitting you're British makes you think you're a sell out. I don't feel that way. It's all in the mind. You can be whoever you think you are. Colour's not even a part of it. Scots, Welsh and Irish people, what are they? Are they British? No one cares about that. In England, there's supposed to be a big divide between north and south. You've got your southern softies and your northern rednecks. And in the north, there's Yorkshire folk and Lancashire folk. They had a war over five hundred years ago and they still haven't forgotten about it to this day. I don't really care about how people want to classify me. It's not important. Paying your bills, bringing your family up and trying to get on with life, that's more important. That's what affects you.

We've always lived in Bradford. My dad came in sixty summat. He came as a single man so he had no worries. I think

26

they were all dead lucky when they came: must have been a right blast. My dad got off the plane, got a bus here to Bradford and on the same day, he got a job: believe that, if you can. In them days you could walk into a mill and they'd set you on. Even if you couldn't speak English, they'd give you a job; that's how plentiful work was. And they were all together, all brothers abroad; they had a strong link between themselves because they were all in the same boat together. The rest is history. Forty years later, here I am – telling you about it.

He went back to Pakistan a few years later, got married to my mum and then came back and carried on working here – same mill, same job. He stuck at that work, in that mill, for as long as he could. He didn't pack it in but they made him redundant: mill closed down. He didn't get much, that's what he says but, with that money and some he borrowed, he did like all the others were doing in them days; bought himself a corner shop. We ran that as a family business for about a good ten/ twelve years. He only learnt to drive because of the shop – for cash and carrying. When we were at school, my mum would stand in the shop and serve. When my mum stood in the shop, my dad went to the cash and carry, paying bills and stuff. When he came back, she'd help him put stuff on shelves and then she'd do the housework – cleaning, cooking, picking my sister up from school. She never got a break from it but neither did my dad. Busy shop, that was. A nice, busy little shop.

We used to do a lot of credit. My dad had this big book under the counter with all the names of the people who owed him money – hundreds of pounds, some of them. They all paid up when he sold it. Had to sell it, really. It was getting too much for him. I didn't want to do it, I wanted to study and he wanted me to study even more. He wanted me to go into sciences, medicine or something like that, something well paid, something with a bit of status. Our people in those days, they had a lot of hopes for their kids. Everyone's parents did: 'My son's going to be a doctor, my son's set to be a barrister, scientist, lawyer.'

My grades weren't good enough, that's my excuse. I took 'A' levels in college but that was a waste of time. College was not a good idea if you were a bit borderline. There were some who did really well but they were focused and their minds were fixed on what they were supposed to be doing. I got tempted and distracted and wasted my time on too much silly stuff. Messing around, not going to classes, girls, cars – silly stuff.

I didn't plan on going into this line of work but it came up and here I am. I got it through the Careers Service. I always liked cars; which young lad doesn't have a thing for cars? I wouldn't say I was a natural mechanic but I picked it up over the years. The mechanics I worked with, they were alright. All white guys in a proper dealership garage. One or two of them were a bit funny, but I didn't cause problems – kept my head down and got on with it, like you do. Did that for a year and they paid for me to go back to college on day-release.

I enjoy the work. A good laugh. You have that camaraderie that you probably don't get in offices and places like that. The work can be boring but that goes with any job. Nowadays we're not really mechanics, just fitters, switch parts around. Now and then, you might actually do a bit of mechanic-ing. The difference between mechanic-ing and fitting is that with mechanic-ing, you have to do a lot more thinking; you're solving problems without the luxury of swapping parts. In Pakistan, there's more mechanics than fitters. In Pakistan, if a clutch plate burns out, they won't go to the parts shop or the dealers and get another one. They'll actually make another one; believe that if you can. If a car has an accident, they'll repair – panel beat – it right back into shape.

I'm thinking of going to Pakistan. Not this year, but the year after. Have to save a bit of money first but I do need a break. I want my kids to see it more than for myself. My wife, it'll only be the second time back for her, too. I've not been back since I got married. Blew me away, when I went the first time. I was put off by a lot of things but I was at the same time drawn to it. Everybody talks about Pakistan so you're always curious. When you get there, it's another world completely.

Life's so cheap there and if you're at the bottom, there's nothing for you except family, if you have any, and charity if you're lucky. Seeing Pakistan makes you appreciate what you've got here. Here, we want for nothing. Even if you've got nothing, there's someone or some service that you can rely on. That's why I want my kids to go there, to see a poor country and to see how hard it is and for them to appreciate how easy and good they've got it here. There's that part, and I want them to learn a bit about their culture, their other culture. It's about your roots. To know where you're going in life, you should know where you've come from. It's not the most important thing but that place is part of us and this place is part of us.

The youngest one, she's too young to travel yet. Over there if a kid gets ill, it can be difficult getting medical help. I just don't want to risk it. In a year or two she'll be strong enough and big enough to take it on. She'll be starting school but the others, they're already attending. I'll definitely take them during the school holidays. You don't want them missing out on their education. When I was at school, kids would always be going to Pakistan during term time. Teachers would complain about them missing important lessons which is right – made their job harder. It's not worth it. School's important; you can only get the best out of it if you're there.

I remember my first day. Nursery, not school. I remember she dressed me up really nice, my mum. I had these brand new cords and a brand new shirt and a new pair of shoes – all ready for my first day. I thought it was *Eid* – had no idea what school was about. I had a rough picture in my head about it because my mum would mention it without really explaining it a lot: 'You're going to go to school and there you'll read.' Read meaning learn but I thought it was read meaning just read. My dad got the *Daily Jang* every day and he'd read that. So I was thinking school's this place just for me, and me alone, where I'd go to learn to read the *Daily* bloody *Jang*.

So I'm there, and all we're doing is playing with toys and playing around with sand and buckets and spades. There were a few other kids' mothers there as well, and I started to notice that they, the mothers, started dropping off. Every time you looked, another one had left. Some of the kids whose mums had already gone, they were crying buckets. Got me thinking: my mum, she'll probably be next to leave me. So I kept an eye on her as much as I could but even she sneaked out when I wasn't looking. I looked around and she was nowhere. It's funny but I lost it. Crying my little eyes out, I was. The teacher picked me up in her arms and tried calming me down but I couldn't understand a word: this was the first time I'd ever been this close to an English person. How did I know what she was saying? We didn't even have a telly so I couldn't even learn it – English – from there.

There weren't that many Pakistani kids in that class but there was this one girl and she came up and calmed me down. I'll never forget it. She was wearing these little yellow 'bell bottoms' they called them and these bright red shiny shoes. She spoke to me in Pakistani but she sort of told me off, too. I'll never forget, she said, *'Buss kar. Chup kar. Muree atch see, tharee ami, ala. Buss kar, huhn.'* That shut me up. I thought, 'Yeah, she probably will come back, my mum, won't she? What's the point in crying?' And all those toys, too – you got lost in them, there were that many.

I made friends with her, that girl. We went through first school together in the same class but then we went to different middle schools. I've seen her a few times over the years – in town, driving a car, doing her shopping. I even spoke to her once when I was at college and she remembered me. She was married and everything the last time I saw her and that was over a decade ago. It is a small world, they say. Small town, if you think about – everyone knows everyone in this place.

Kids don't have language as a problem any more. They're born speaking English. It's everywhere, all around them, so it comes naturally. Take my kids, all three of them speak perfect English, better than I speak it and better than they speak our own language. With me they speak English but with their mum, it's all in Pakistani. Best of both worlds. I think there's no point in learning Urdu as a written language – what use is it? Everyone uses English nowadays, even in Pakistan. My wife, she can read and write it because that's how she was schooled in Pakistan, but over here, there's no call for it that I can see. I'm not saying it's not a good thing, it's good to learn any language in that way, but in this country especially, something like Urdu is looked on differently to French, Spanish or Russian. It's seen as not a valuable thing. I still want them to speak Punjabi so they can communicate with their elders: a bit of wisdom won't harm them. It's another language and it's about their parents and about themselves, in a way.

I'd like to retire in about ten to fifteen years. That's why I work so much. Everybody wants to retire at a younger age but the government keeps telling everyone they'll have to work until they drop. With us, it's a bit harder. My kids, when they're old enough and when they're ready, their marriages will have to be funded by us. My wife doesn't work which leaves me as the breadwinner. To some people it's an odd thing to be thinking of at my age. I have to work hard if I stand a chance of getting the things I want in ten or twenty years time. There's the garage wage which pays for everything like bills, mortgage and the usual expenses. But I'm doing something on the side as well which is helping me build up a little nest egg. My wife, she takes care of the house really well and manages to squirrel some away into a *committee* which is there for us whenever we want it. Kids are expensive but that's part of life. Once they've been wedded off, that's our headache over and done with. After that, they can look after themselves.

I didn't want to get married. I don't think anyone wants to get married but I knew it had to happen soon. I was twenty, twenty-two, something like that. My wife, she was a year or two younger than me. I saw her twice before we were married: once in a photograph and once in person and that was for about a second. My marriage was okay. I had friends who were what I'd call forced. With me, I went over to Pakistan knowing what was in store. My mum and dad didn't lie or hide my passport or anything silly like that. One of my friends went over for a holiday and he came back in tears, married and everything at eighteen years old. At that time I thought, 'Fair enough, I've had a fair innings as a single man – go for it.' I can't complain and I never have. We're happy. We were never not happy. We've got kids. We talk, we get on and we've got our lives together. But that's not what I'll do with our kids when their time comes. We'll be there for them and we'll manage it for them but I don't want to impose anything. My wife and me, we talk about this. She thinks a bit differently to me. She's from Pakistan and so she's got one eye on over there. She's got nephews and nieces and people are thinking of matching them up already but I don't want that to happen. There's no future in that. It won't happen because I'm against it and our kids will be, too.

Kids today, they know what they want and they've got more knowledge about these things than I ever did. Some of the stuff they come out with puts me to shame. Stuff about anything, really: about life, about politics and especially about Islam. Even if you wanted to force your kids into a marriage, they'd turn around and tell you you're sinning. A friend of mine, that's what his eldest daughter said to him, 'You can't do a forced marriage in Islam, Dad. It's not recognised as a marriage if there's force.' He told me he felt like a clown. He just shut up because he knew she was right.

I'd like to be a bit more religious. You get so bogged down into work and money, not the important things – the really important things – like remembering Allah, like living in the way of Allah. You put those on the back-burner. Keep putting it off, but you can't keep doing that forever. Our kids do more than me and they know more than me. Over the last year or two I've thought about it more and more. Some of my friends and relatives have been going on *Hajj* and they're all better and happier when they come back.

I'll definitely stay in Bradford. Born here and I'll end up dying here, too. Where else would you go? That's not the question, really. The question is – why would you go anywhere else? I've never wanted for anything in this town. Anything I've ever wanted, I've got. It's not perfect, but which place is? No matter where you go there'll be problems. The youngsters and the riots, that happened, but there were reasons why they happened and got out of control. I'm glad I'm not a youngster now because if it was me, I'd be inside now. Kids, that's all: don't think, act silly and if they get you on camera, you pay the price.

The things that annoy me are the normal things that you see every day: dirt on the streets – the litter and the tipping – and the dirt that lives in the council, lining their own pockets and blowing up their own egos. That really pisses me off. If Bradford was a firm or a business, then it would have gone bust or the bosses would have been sacked or something would have happened a long time ago. Instead, the councillors are busy getting their pictures in the *T&A*, smiling their tits off. But nobody really talks about that. Bradford's known for curries and rioting but it's more than that. With Bradford, it's all out there in the open. There's no dirty secrets lingering around; it can be a rough place but it's always an honest one. I'm talking about the normal people, now. We haven't got big ideas or illusions about ourselves – we don't believe we're anything more than what we are.

Accents

Near the end of eighty-seven, my dad came to Bradford and started working for my uncle. I was too young to remember too much about Birmingham. If I go back, it doesn't seem like home. I was born there but that's about it. When I first moved here I used to live up near Leeds Road. I was at Tyersal First School for two years because we moved up to Heaton in eighty-nine. I felt out of place because I didn't speak the same; I had a bit of a Brummie accent. Even now I don't think I speak the same as lads from Bradford. I haven't got a regional Bradfordian accent. My brother speaks with a proper accent but only when he's with his mates. When we're at home, then it's different. My sisters, they have very middle-class sort of accents.

My sisters had a lot of white friends when they came here from Birmingham. They went to uni, got their degrees, came back, worked. One of my sisters is working at college, another is a teacher. Our family outlook is not 'you lot should study' and 'you lot should get married'. My parents are saying, 'You're free to do what you want; if you want to aspire to do whatever, then do it.'

My eldest sister, she's not married. She says, 'I want to be self-made. I want my own house. I want my own car.' She'll be about thirty this year – a bit old, and that's a bit of a taboo issue. With our cousins it's an issue. One of my cousins – we were just chatting about marriage and that – and he said, 'So, when's she going to get married?'

I said, 'Whenever she wants.'

He goes, 'But people talk.'

'Well, people can talk whatever they want.'

That's the thing, even my parents are like that: 'What are people going to think?' That's why I want to move away; that way I wouldn't have any of this politics. I don't want my kids and my wife to get involved in family politics. It's just not healthy. You have this person who's not speaking to that person because that person's said something to the other person. I just can't do with that.

My mum's friends, they find it really weird that when I get up in the morning I make my own breakfast. They're like, 'How does he do that?' They'll be in the kitchen chatting to my mum. I'm hungry and I'll walk in and make myself something to eat. They find that really weird: 'Why is he in the kitchen?' My sister says to me, 'I'm glad you're like that because your wife will thank your mum afterwards. At least he does something for himself.' That's why I don't need a Pakistani wife. Pakistani wives, we have this conception that they're like robots. You say, 'make tea,' and it's made, 'make dinner,' and it's made. I want mutualness, that's the way I've been raised.

My cousins still live up Leeds Road. They were a bit weird to me at first because I don't live up here with them in the *'hood*. There's a lot of black culture there. They all watch too many hip hop videos: 'We're living in like Compton'. It's nowhere near. I don't know why it is but they just seem to think that it's cool. They aspire to be like that. I used to find myself feeling like an outsider. It got to a point where I used to say to them that I was raised here, I came here when I was five years old, I've lived on this street. You try to grasp something that keeps you on the inside.

When I moved here there was only one other family of Asians on the street. But now, over the course of fifteen years, it's mainly Asians. Leeds Road, it's more traditional, like back home, like Pakistan. If you live in a village, everyone knows everyone else. They come up to your house, you go to theirs, they have time for you; it's at that level. Where I live now, everything's a bit more spaced out, more of a boundary. Me, in my street, hardly anybody knows me. At first I used to think it was security, but it's not. You're more secure in an environment where everyone knows each other. So if your house gets robbed the chances are somebody would see it or do something about it. Stuff like drugs and kids messing about on the streets, you don't get so much of that in my area; you don't have it to the same extent as you do there. I don't know why it's different because you've got the same people, the same communities but living in different areas.

Every time I go to a big city or on holiday I realise that when you're in Bradford your thinking's quite blinkered. You don't see the outside world. It feels like you're in Bradford and that's all there is. Some of my mates up Leeds Road get excited when they have to go into Leeds because they never leave Bradford. That's a Yorkshire thing; maybe some of that's rubbed off on us without us even realising. My cousin's wife's from Pakistan, she's been here three or four years. Every time they come up from London, his wife says, 'Let's go here, let's go there, everything's here in Bradford.' When they come they love it: 'It's like Pakistan. You don't do nothing here. Life's so slow.'

I've been to Pakistan. When people go they live in their village and they just stay there. They might go out for a day but that's it. I went with a guy who was always going over and coming back. He says to me, 'You're my guest because you're coming over with me, so you stay at my house and it's up to me to take you everywhere. This is my country and I'm going to show you what it's really like.' You get a lot of kids who've been to Islamabad but they've only been to the airport; they haven't really seen the city.

I want to travel all over the world. I've been to France, Germany, Holland. Been to Dubai for holidays. There's so many different places to go now: the Far East, South America. I never travelled until about nineteen ninety-nine. I got my passport renewed and my dad goes to me, 'Look, you've got a passport, make sure you use it as much as you can. The world is your mosque so you should travel as much as you can and you should try to take good from everywhere that you go.' After that, every year I've got to go somewhere. This year I haven't been anywhere and I'm dying to go. Spain – Barcelona – that's my favourite place. I just fell in love with it the first time I went. An amazing place. It's similar to Dubai, the lifestyle. Very chilled out. Next time I go I want to go down south and see the Alhambra, see some of the Moorish Muslim places. In the south of Spain there's amazing mosques.

The first time I went was about three or four years ago. My sisters and one of their mates went for like a weekend from

Thursday to Monday. Everyone was chilled out, everything's open 'til late, and there's a very laid back atmosphere. When we first got there I said, 'We're going to have to find a curry house. We'll have to get *roti* tonight.' My sisters wear full *hijab* and *jilbab* so with them I did feel a little self-conscious. With me they can't tell. I'd go into a shop and people would chat Spanish to me, but I'd be like, 'No, I'm not Spanish.' So I was cool, I was happy, I fit right in. With my sisters it was different. I don't know how they felt but I felt a bit uncomfortable about how certain people were – how they'd look. After a while you realise that they weren't looking in a negative way. They were just curious. I'd been to Spain about three times and my mum says to me, 'I'm sure you've got a girl there!'

I'm worried about Asian girls, Muslim girls, here. You get the very straight pious women, decent women, but yet a lot of them are worse than I was. My mum says, 'You should get married to someone from Pakistan.' And I'm saying, 'No, we can't. We're totally different, we're not compatible. Their culture's that and our culture's this. We have washing machines and they have a river.'

I always say stuff like this to my mum and she gets really pissed off, but she does understand where I'm coming from. My mum mentions it a lot because she's teasing. Saying that, I remember when I was in Pakistan when I was fifteen or sixteen. My parents were here, and my grandma there was saying, 'You should get married.' I'm like sixteen and she's like, 'So? So what? Get married.'

My uncle there, he's got this scam, he goes, 'This is what you do. You go, "Yeah, I want to get married." Get engaged, even get married, but don't get her a visa! Come back to Pakistan every year for about three years. Chill out in England, and chill out in Pakistan.'

When I get married I don't want to mess about whatsoever. I was sixteen and I said to him, 'That's totally not right.'

It's the grandmas, they're the funniest. They start blackmailing you, giving it, 'I want to see you get married, I'm going to die soon, and I want to see you get married.'

I just said, 'If it's Allah's will, it's Allah's will. I can't do anything about that. I'm sorry, but I can't do nothing about you dying or not.'

I was talking to a cousin of mine who's the same age as me and he's at university and he's going to graduate next year. We were at this wedding together and we went outside for a cig break and I started talking to him.

'Do you think about marriage?'

He goes, 'No, not really.'

'Listen, you've got to think about this because next year when you graduate, your parents are going to come down on you. Believe it or not they're going to say it to you, aren't they? They're going to say, "You've done your uni, you've done your studying, you have to get married. Think about what you want to do."'

He goes, 'I don't know.'

I said, 'Well have you got any ideas? Do you want to get married from back home? Do you want to get married from here?'

The truth is, I was only saying that to him because I was trying to think of myself as well, because I'm in the same

44

position as him. And the truth is, none of us has a clue because in a year's time they're going to be saying this to us: 'You're going to get married.'

I pray five times a day. I've only started practicing quite recently. I started thinking that I want to move to Spain, and I thought, 'Well, can I?' Well, Islam's not a culture. You've got Muslims in Morocco, you've got Muslims in Pakistan, a big community of Muslims in the south of Spain. And they all live different lives and they have different cultures, but they still have this shared thing of Islam. They have that same belief, what their obligations are; they know what's not right. But they still live their lives wherever they are. Islam's international; it's not peculiar to one part of the world. It's not a culture and that's the thing. It's a total way of life. Based on that I could easily move to Spain. It can't be that hard.

The world's changed and nowadays it might be an issue. Travelling itself is something: are they going think I'm a terrorist, to bang me up because I've got a *Qur'an* in my bag? I've got friends who know about this stuff and they were telling me the best places to live as a Muslim are the places where Islam is there top to bottom, and also those places where there is no Islam. That's where you can set an example. I've yet to actually read about that country that's Islamic top to bottom or even know of one. If you're a Muslim you can probably do more good here than you could as a Muslim in Saudi or somewhere. Now more than ever, that's probably quite necessary.

Different Values

I went to Pakistan in nineteen ninety-five. My father went over to build himself a house. The general idea was to go back and live back home. I'd just started my 'A' levels and my father asked me to come over in the summer holidays – 'Come over, we haven't seen you for such a long time.'

I left and I spent sixteen months there; didn't complete my first year. My education, I couldn't really get into it when I came back, plus most of my friends were already at university. I did 'A' levels at Bradford College and within two or three months I left. I'd have loved to have gone to university and got a degree in something but that's not how things worked out.

I'd never been there before. It was a big eye-opener for me in terms of what Pakistan was about. One of the first things that hit me was poverty. I'd never seen poverty in my life. In this country, we were aware of poverty and stuff, what we'd seen on television and through the media, but to actually see it, that was a big eye-opener. It made me think about the culture and the lack of closeness.

We're brought up on different values. Here, a friend is someone who you choose to be your friend. Back home, a friend is somebody within the family. You only can hold a friendship with your cousin or your relative. If it's somebody outside your caste or your family, then you see them with a different eye, you see them with a business agenda, or something else. You don't really see them as a friend as in somebody who you spend time with. I realised that this is how the village was divided. People would only associate themselves with you if you were from a certain caste. It's something that was in your face on a daily basis.

I haven't got good memories of Pakistan. I enjoyed the sun and it was a very relaxed environment. Nobody really works. You come out of the house, walk into the bazaar and they're all leaning about. A lot of money was going from here and people didn't need to work. We were supporting them. I didn't understand that one little bit. My father helped quite a few families and they were so ungrateful: 'I build you a house to live in, I send you money every month for you to feed your kids and to send to school. And from that money, you set up a little business or buy some property.' They were like Lord-of-the-Manor kind of people: 'We did everything and this is off our own bat.' And you think, 'Yeah, I'm sure you really set all this up.'

My father went back and he built himself a villa. Spent a bit of money, and in this little village it showed. Almost half the village turned against him. You could see it in people's eyes that they didn't like it. I didn't like that. If somebody supported me, even for two or thee years, I'd show my appreciation to this person. But I didn't see any of that.

People have gone back to Pakistan and married there, whether it's a male or a female, and their marriage is successful. As long as there's compatibility between the two people, fair enough. I got married a couple of years ago. I wanted to get married and I wanted a partner who I could spend my life with. She's from here, down south, within the family. My wife had to be compatible to me. I knew my wife as a teenager, as a relative and a cousin, so when the prospect came up, it wasn't as daunting. I actually knew some of her background and stuff. So that was a positive for me.

Arranged marriages, I don't think they are wrong, but I think there's a process there and as long as that process has been followed, then I think arranged marriage for a Muslim is probably the only way to get married. When I talk about a process I mean that you have contact with this person beforehand and you have a chance to discuss things. I know a lot of guys, a lot of friends, that have got married to keep their family happy. They needed somebody to help and support their parents, to maybe even keep them company. They've got married for this reason and they're happy with that. Some of these marriages have worked. I am talking about a male here who will get married because his parents have asked him to get married and he knows that this person he is getting married to will look after his parents. And he's happy with that and he'll get on with it and that's fine. The whole argument falls back on what you want out of this marriage. What are you looking for? Your parents saying that you're going to get married to this person no matter what; I don't understand this. That's not arranged to me, that's forced.

I've got no kids of my own at the moment. Kids are always a good thing. Everybody knows that it's a big bad world out here, because we live it. You feel a bit protective. What really brings it home is that you know you can't protect kids because you're aware of the environment, the society around you. You know your kid's going to go out and play. You don't know who he's getting involved with at the end of the street. I think that's what really brings it home. I can't really protect my kid. You've got to send him away to school, you've got to let him out of the house. As a kid, I got involved, met all sorts of different people who had a lot of influence on me.

One big issue for me, especially with my nephews and nieces: playing in the back street, the back alley. I grew up in back alleys. I know what back alleys are about, I know that it's happening now; it will be happening in twenty years. You get into fights, you swear, you go on missions smashing people's windows, or nicking something from a garden, you know. And I didn't want my nephews and nieces being part of that. We've got a back garden and we built a massive gate and put a padlock on it so that they have to play in the garden and couldn't go outside, just to protect them from the back alleys kind of scenario.

I've got a niece who were bullied at school. I've never experienced being bullied. I don't know what bullying feels like. She was a really quiet kid, and I thought that was because of this bullying. It really changed this child in terms of her character and everything. Because she was, up to the age of say five – until she went to school – a very bubbly child. A couple of years at school and she turned into this very, very, quiet, mundane kind of child, and that had a bit of an effect on me. How much can we protect a child? If she didn't go to school, or she didn't get bullied, maybe she would have been a completely different person in terms of her character.

I have a nephew who goes to a mosque and apart from teaching Arabic they teach Islamic studies. They teach history lessons about prophets and morals and ethics and stuff like this. There was none of this ten years ago. There is a complete classroom where they break it up. It is happening now. I couldn't vouch for all mosques, but I am aware of quite a lot that are doing it. That's something that definitely has improved. As a young kid we were always told that 'There's God' but I didn't really understand the concept of what God is. That's something that I've taught myself. I didn't have no Islamic influences from the mosque, no Islam. Just went there, learned Arabic and came back.

As a kid I was a big lad and I used to get into a lot of fights. My PE teacher says to me, 'You should take up some sort of activity because you've got a lot of energy in you. Take up boxing.' So I joined a boxing club, did eight to twelve weeks training or something. And then they put me up for a little fight. But the thing that I never really understood was that in boxing you don't fight your age, you fight your weight. And because I was a big lad, as an eleven/twelve year old, I were fighting fifteen/sixteen year olds. This one fight was with a fifteen/sixteen year old and he hammered the hell out of me.

I met this one guy there who inspired me to start training and stuff. And he had a big influence on me. And this lad, later on, turned out to be a big criminal. And that had a lot of influence on me as well because he was a bit of a thug and a gangster. Because I had these influences, some of my tendencies were of a thug and a gangster, as well. That could have been so easily me. I had a chance about six months ago to actually meet this person who I hadn't met for a long time. I brought this up. He'd seen me with a beard, I'm practicing, and he hinted that it could have been him so easily; both of us were on the same path.

From fourteen to sixteen, most teenagers go through a phase, they're a bit rebellious, feel like they own the world, can do anything. That's how I felt as a fourteen year old. To parents, to our elders, to everybody, especially authority I was like, 'Yeah, man. I can do what I want and there's no one to stop me.' Whatever we wanted to do we could. As long as people come out of that phase and develop themselves, that's fine. But what worries me is when people don't; when you get twenty-five year olds or twenty-six year olds still acting, still behaving like that.

Young lads hanging about at the end of street getting into a bit of mischief is always a concern. It's getting more and more dangerous and more and more criminal. When we were young we did a lot of bad things; we probably didn't even understand them at the time, the consequences, how bad we were. It's nothing unique to the Asian youths. Let's say I was born and raised in a white community. I would have done everything that I did within an Asian community. That's how this environment brought us up. I don't believe we did anything different. We hung about in groups or gangs on street corners. If I was white I would have still done that.

The time I spent in West Bowling was the age of eight 'til thirteen or fourteen. You get out of the house, go to school, come back, go to mosque, come back, play a little bit of football and you're into your bed. That's all it was in them years. If I was living anywhere else, it would have been the same.

Maybe now it's a lot different in terms of living in a community and actually being involved in a community.

I haven't always been religious. I learned my religion in terms of what religion is and what it's asking me to do, and then how I'm going about doing it. It was a long process. I was at a stage in my life when I was comfortable in myself and I didn't have no real goals or ambition. And then, in kicked the spiritual side. I've got no real big achievements. As youths, we had ambitions like we wanted to be wealthy, successful. I've lost it. I think my religion has a lot to do with it. I'm content with myself to a certain extent, I've got a certain level of happiness. I would like to live in a Muslim country but I'm happy as long as I can practice my religion. This environment is comfortable for me. I can wear a beard, I can wear Asian dress, comfortably walk the streets, go about and do my business and live my daily life, and it's not an issue. This is something that I have actually put a bit of thought into. I think it is specific to Bradford. Because the same people are living with Asians or have lived with Asians for so many years, they understand. The bridges are a bit closer than maybe in some other communities.

I'm religious now in terms of I'm a practicing Muslim. I try to obey the religion wherever it's possible. I refuse to get a mortgage because of the interest. The interest thing is one issue, another thing is that it's commitment. To get a mortgage, I'm committed and I'm stuck: I can't do nothing for twenty-five years. One of the reasons I left my previous job was because of the nine-to-five thing – the rut of it. I don't like it, it's this whole thing of being in a system.

Naraazgee

Things went too far. Unbearable all round, it got. But my conscience is clean; I sleep at night no bother at all. I left them because there was no other choice. I'd like to think I'm better off on my own but I can't say that I feel that way about it. It might turn out to be one of those moves that I regret for the rest of my life. It's been over a year since I left but it still feels sort of new. You get used to some of it but you miss a lot of it, too; family life had been everything for nearly all your life and then one day it's all changed. It's a big thing. It's not something you can get used to so quickly.

I saw it coming. I told them about it a good four/five years before it happened. I warned them but they didn't take any notice. It started with my brother; six years above me. He were born in seventy-three, I was born in seventy-nine. They got him married when he was about twenty. His missus, she's from Pakistan – usual story and all that. He didn't want to get married at all. It's happened to a few people that way. Parents forced them into marriage and they didn't live happily ever after. My brother, he's married and he's miserable and so's his wife. I tell them straight, that I'm not going out like that. They got another thing coming if they think they can try that on with me. I'm fifteen when I tell them the first time. When I'm eighteen/nineteen, the subject comes up again and I'm like, 'No way'.

Last year, they started again like they do every year but now it's big time, real serious, a lot of pressure. 'You're getting old. You have to do it soon before you get too old so you might as well do it now.' And me, I'm saying, 'I'm young. I'm not old. I'm like twenty-two years.' But they keep at it.

My brother gets involved and says they should learn from him because him and his missus, they're still not like a proper married husband and wife should be. My brother says, 'What's the point? It's not good, doing it like that because the only ones who want it are them, not the people who are important; the ones who are supposed to be getting married.' Even his missus, she says the same thing, too. Ends up like everyone on one side or on the other. My mum and dad start getting ideas that we're all against them. They say to my brother and his missus, 'You're our enemies, now.' You'd think they were having a laugh, but they were dead serious about it all. Proper *naraazgee*. In the end I'd had enough. I just got my shit together – few clothes and that, bits and bats, some music, some money and chipped.

I'm alright where I am at the moment. It's alright, the area, but it's not the same as Heaton and Manningham where I grew up. That's my real *'hood*. I got a pad round here on purpose. There were flats and that going over there – there's more in Manningham than round here – but I didn't want to stay round there, with it being so close to home and my mum and dad. Didn't want to cause trouble. My dad, the last thing he said to me was, 'Don't come near my door ever again. After today, it's over.' So I thought, better get out of his way, better chip somewhere else.

At first I wanted to leave town altogether. I've got mates who've got contacts with people from other places – Oldham, Leeds, Manchester. Even thought about chipping down Birmingham. Supposed to be a lot happening there work-wise, chilling wise. Bradford's Bradford. Didn't feel right. I couldn't do it. I thought about all those places but at the end I thought, 'I'm not gonna be in Bradford and that's a bad idea.' I've left home – my family – which is bad, but leaving Bradford, that's summat else. It's home and it's yours, too. It's not just a place where you have an address. It's a part of you, something you've grown up with. Bradford's mine, my town and that means we sort of know each other. I won't say I know all of it inside out but the Bradford that I do know, I know it as well as I know my own self. Without it, I wouldn't be me. I don't think I'd ever leave. The funny thing is, Bradford might as well be the whole world for me. Nearly everyone that I've ever known is in Bradford.

First week I stayed with my mates – one night here, couple of nights there. By then I did some tracking and got this place sorted. Had a bit of money, borrowed a bit of money, bought a bit of stuff – furniture and that – and moved in straight away.

I'd be nothing without my mates. We have a laugh together but it's more than that. Me, I'm a case in point: when I were first sorting this place out, they helped with money and all that. 'It's a mate so you've got to help him out.' Who else do you have? I have relatives but I don't know them like I know my mates. *Biradari* to me means nothing. I know what it is but it's not important to me, doesn't make any difference because I don't see the world that way. People like my dad, for them it's important because it's about who you are. Who you are is who you know and a lot of the ones you know are in your *biradari*. For me, who I am is who I know as well. I know my friends and I still know my family even though they might not want to know me. Us lot, my mates and that, we don't even mention *biradari*. Take for example your dad talking to someone and you know, the word might pop in conversation somewhere, 'Oh, so and so, he's our *biradari na bandah*' or 'No, they're not our *biradari*'. But us lot, when we're talking, we'll say he's from over Leeds Road way or from Manningham or he knows or flexes with someone that we know. That's how we know who someone is. If I ever said it - 'Which *biradari* is he in?' - my mates, they'd think I'd gone a bit mental.

I'm hoping things will change between me and my mum and dad. Physically, I can survive for the rest of my life without them but mentally it's different. They're your parents. They bring you into the world and they do everything they can to make your life easy and good. I know that. But it was a big thing they were wanting from me. It was a wrong thing they were asking of me.

I know this woman, about same age as me. I knew her from school and she was a right good lass – used to tell me to not mess around and to work hard but I never listened. A nice religious lass, now. Not a slapper or anything like that. Like a sister, I'd say. She were telling me about her situation a bit back. Just like my brother's, because her parents made her get married when she didn't want to. She got married and lived with the guy for about two years but they couldn't get on. In the end she just divorced him. And now she's living on her own because her parents want nothing to do with her because she did that and the whole *biradari* business got into it. It's obvious – they shouldn't have made her marry him in the beginning.

The best thing is that it's made her a better person, Islamically speaking. She's got a lot of knowledge now and that's what she turned to while she were having a rough time. Very religious and proper. She's the one who told me that both people getting married have to be happy and willing to get married because if they're not, then it's not really classed as a marriage.

I can't understand it because there's nothing good about doing that to your own kids. You wouldn't even do that to somebody else's kids. I would never do that to mine if I ever have any. I would like to get married and have the kids. I'm not planning on it but I hope it happens. Inside, in my heart, I want to make up and get back with my parents. I never wanted to not get married but not at that time and not to that person. Before thirty would be good and to someone from here, anywhere in Britain. A Muslim woman, you know, someone I could get on with. Someone I could be married to properly.

Rat Race

I lived in London for a year. I went out, I did my work, I didn't have any contact with anybody. I didn't have any friends there or nothing. If I'd have wanted to I could have got to know people, made friends. It doesn't matter where you live, you always get to know people. But London life, it's a different kind of life altogether, you can't compare it to Bradford. When you're in London it's a rat race: just work, work, work.

There's a lot of people who work like dogs all their lives. I haven't got any plans, I just take every day as it comes. You look around Bradford and there's a lot of old set-ups. Everywhere you look, everybody's doing something; if they aren't doing something then they're thinking of doing something, wired up to do something else. I've got friends who are working in a factory; they're also planning something else as a sideline or something as a business venture. It's all about making money. Making more and more money. Maybe that's something that we've always been interested in.

The difference is now we're settled here so we're alright to spend it as well. My dad sends money back to the family in Pakistan and we just have this sort of big family pot. We don't really have *my* money and *his* money – we all sort of contribute to everything. In effect we all end up sending money back to Pakistan. As long as my dad's alive we don't really have a choice. I wouldn't send it back if it was up to me because they're not worthy of it. If something happened to one of my friends, I'd feel more hurt or emotionally upset than I would if my cousin died in Pakistan. We don't know them. You don't know them by saying, 'He's my cousin.'

I don't like the mentality of Pakistanis that come from over there. My dad's done whatever he's done for them but we're his family. We feel upset that he'll bend backwards to see they're okay. To them, their uncle – their *mawa* – or whatever he is to them, he doesn't mean 'owt. As long as he keeps sending them money. And when he doesn't send them anything it's, 'What have you ever done for us?' That story goes with all of us. They've all built houses back home and propped their brothers and mothers and sisters and uncles and aunts, but they all piss on them in the end. We won't have no regrets like that. We don't want to take that privilege away from him. Dad's lived his life, he's given us a good upbringing and that, and, if he feels happy by helping his family, then who are we? Why should we say anything? It's not as if he's saying, 'Give me your money. I'll send your money.' He's paid his dues, he's paid his taxes and he gets his own pension or whatever. Because he's living with us brothers he's got no expenditure. So whether he wants to send five thousand pounds or twenty thousand pounds, he doesn't need to explain himself. And it's okay: 'But the day you go, *the day you go*, that's it – we won't be sending nothing.'

Things are changing. Them that come over get out-classed. They can see that they're getting rejected by the husbands or wives from here. But then the mother-in-law or the father-in-law, they try to kind of push it along and let things carry on, until it gets to breaking point. It's like this house that I've got. I've had *mangaythurs* living there. They won't have been in the country three or five years. They've all got the same mentality which is: 'Let the wife work. With the money she gets she should buy a house, she should pay the bills, she should do the house up to her own taste. The money that I get, I'll give her housekeeping – forty/fifty pounds a week – and I should have thirty/forty pounds for my own spending money, and the rest I should send back to my mum and my dad and my brothers and sisters – let them build a house.' But our girls, they don't want that because for them their home is here.

Those guys, you see them and they cry. They come and they say, 'We want a room on rent.' They're getting booted out by their wives or the in-laws; they get divorced, or separated. Once they're separated that's it, the girl doesn't want to know. Money's an aspect, that's one thing, then there's compatibility. They're not on the same wavelength. They can't joke, they can't laugh, talk to each other and they are genuinely sad people. But they've all got these similarities, they've all got one way of thinking. It's still that Pakistani thing. Most people's dad, they've been here forty/fifty years. They left that country still a young man, maybe twenty-five years old. Up until recently they've always thought that way – 'We'll live in a house, but we'll help people as well – our brothers our sisters, families.' My dad, to this day, he still thinks like that. And that's how they are, them that come from Pakistan. Because we've spent all our lives here, we think, 'What do we earn all this money for if we're not going to spend it on ourselves?' We're not going to spend it on them, are we?

I went to pick up my sister a fortnight ago from Manchester Airport. The last time I went to Manchester Airport must have been a good five years ago. And a good five years ago, Pakistanis would only go to Pakistan. You go to Manchester Airport, London Airport, Heathrow, Gatwick, whichever one you'd go to you'd see queues. Two Pakistanis were going to Pakistan and there would be ten others with them. Where are they going? They're going to Pakistan. I went to Manchester Airport's arrivals. No flights from Pakistan – all from European countries – and there were a load of these Pakistanis and I was thinking, 'There must be a flight from Pakistan coming back.' But there wasn't – they were coming from Turkey! So now the youngsters of today they want to go out, they want to chill out. My sister went for a week, three or four of them, her friends from work. They had a good time and the way they look at it, that's what they're here for. They had a good time, they relaxed, chilled out, had a good experience, saw the sights. That's what you see nowadays. You go to any Pakistani's house, they spend the money on themselves. The houses are lavish, they've got a lot of money, a good lifestyle, good cars. When we see all these kids driving new cars we think they're all drug dealers, but they're not, they just want to live their life.

Drugs in the Pakistani community as a business thing or a venture is no more common than it is for white people. If the government wanted to stop it they could. It wouldn't be difficult, but they need a cycle. It's a good problem to have. It's a problem they want to have, keeps everybody on their toes and keeps the cycle going on. It gets me sometimes. There's a young lad driving a flashy car – Subaru, Mitsubishi, whatever – and people immediately think, 'He's a drug dealer.' They're not all drug dealers but there is still this image. If you see a young twenty-two year old driving a fifteen/twenty thousand pound car, he's a drug dealer, but what people don't realise is his old man isn't sending money back to Pakistan like his grandad did. And that young kid, he may be earning a couple of hundred pounds a week anyway. Affording an expensive car doesn't become such an issue then.

The benefit of Bradford is that everything's at hand. You've lived here all your life, you know people, you feel comfortable. A small close-knit community – even if you farted they know you farted. You don't have to tell anyone anything, they'll find out anyway.

Where we used to have our shop was a small area, a couple of hundred houses. I can remember this one young lad. His dad came to the shop and he says, 'Oh, we send these to school, so they get educated and what have you. I clipped him the other day for being rude. So he goes, "Hit me a little bit harder so that you put a bruise on my body somewhere."'

He was nine years old his son, and this is the son saying to the dad, 'Hit me a little bit harder so I get a red mark on my body and I'll show it to my teacher and they'll lock you up.' This is a nine year old lad talking to his dad.

His dad goes, 'I got scared. I don't want social services taking five kids away.'

If I went to school, was disrespectful to my teacher and my dad found out, I'd get beaten for being rude to my teacher. Nowadays it's changed. The kids are so rude. They tell the

71

teachers where to go, the teachers are scared in case they say summat wrong to them and the parents will be down, 'What have you been saying to my daughter? What have you been saying to my son?' They're so protective. There's no discipline. Giving or creating discipline in kids teaches them a lot of things. When we went to school we did everything, but we always had fear at home. We'd never be rude to teachers in that way. We had a laugh and a joke and we'd be naughty and that, but we'd get punishment. They don't get nothing now. They want everything, they want money, they want labelled clothes. Were we the same? Is this just history repeating itself? Is it the same old thing, or are these today just doing the same things that we did but only doing them differently? Is this just rebelliousness, is this just about young people being young people? Young lads are loud. Were we loud? I see them as a different breed in terms of attitude. Maybe the difference is that when we grew up, although we were mischievous — we'd go out, go shoplifting at the supermarket and things like that — we'd still have fear of getting caught or getting found out. We might have fucked about, we might have had attitude, we might have done dodgy things, but when we saw an older person or a parent we knew where the line was. And there was a line. Now there's no line and I don't know why that is.

Cultural Problems

I were born here but l don't belong. I don't feel like I belong like some people feel they belong. I don't belong to Pakistan, either. I've never been to Pakistan so how can I belong to it? I'm more at home here than anywhere else because this is the only place I know but I don't belong here like I'd belong to a club or a clique. When I say I don't belong here, it's not me that says that; it's not down to me. I might want to belong but that doesn't mean people will let me. When we say British, you think white people. You're still not made to feel it, that you're a part of it all – being British. I'm an outsider, we're outsiders. I don't want to say we're left out or no one likes us or anything like that but we're like aliens from another planet. Some people treat us or see us that way and we might as well be.

At school there were some teachers who said it, in a sly, clever way about us being not the same. Still now it happens, this. Even the ones who were okay used to sort of assume it because they were trying to be nice and help out. Some of them, they're genuinely nice but even them, they can't help it. Any time anything happened, and they were like, 'Is it 'cos you got cultural problems?', 'Don't your parents understand you?', 'Yeah, we understand. It's your culture, isn't it? It's hard being in two cultures, innit?' That kind of stuff. Everything about us was about us as pakis, not normal people because we weren't normal people, weren't the same people. Most of them didn't bother me and I didn't bother them. I don't know if they were racist but they just cruised through – they didn't give a damn so we didn't, either. I left school with hardly nowt worth writing home about. My own fault. Hold my hands up, but a better school would have made a difference.

Five-O's worse. Nothing hidden or clever or sly going on there. With teachers and normal people, they try to hide it, disguise it. They might hate your guts, but still they'll be nice to your face. If you go into a shop or a business or a bank or something it's, 'Sir this and Sir that, please, thank you.' But them, they don't even try to hide it. They don't have to because they got backup – they're the law and what they say goes, no questions asked. Some of them are like proper racist: paki this, paki that. One even swore at me once just while he was talking to me – just like in normal sort of conversation. 'Where are you coming from?' And I said, 'From school,' because I was.

Then he gives it to me, 'Oh yeah? What's a black bastard like you doing in school? How come you're not out dealing?'

Stuff like that happens regular. They do it because they can. They're more than the law because they think they're above it. There's plenty round here, now. Coppers everywhere. Every day I see a copper, nearly. I got nothing to worry about. I don't break the law or 'owt but I do worry about it because you get pulled, stopped, hassled all the time. For nothing. For being there. For wearing what you're wearing, for looking like you're looking, for just being there. If they were proper coppers, if they were fair and didn't hassle you for nothing, then that'd be a good thing. I never had one what I'd call okay *do* with a copper. Always been hassle. They don't know me but they always jump to conclusions about you – you're a paki so you're easy pickings and that. It's a fact of life.

I live in West Bowling, I like it. People from outside, they think it's probably rubbish. If you come to our street, you'll see it's not like that in any way. It's nearly all our own people but that's because white people have been moving out for donkey's years. I'm eighteen now but I remember when I was younger, about five or six, and it was becoming a more and more *aapna* area even in them days. I don't know why them people moved out. I can't believe they were all racist and didn't like living around here. There are a few white people still living here and they're sound. There are some who do get up to no good, but mainly it's a bit settled now compared to what it used to be like.

There's this old *buddee*, an old grandmother. She's really nice. I talk to her but you get some of us who are stupid and give her grief for nothing – just because she's old and English and white or whatever. I've known her since I was a nipper so we sort of know each other in that way. She's lived here all her life. Most of her old friends have moved away but even still, she's not moving. She's got a son and a daughter, all grown up with their own families, and they come up to see her now and then with their kids. She were talking to me the other day about it. Her son, he's telling her to move. Him and her daughter, they're both giving it, 'Sell the house and come live near us.' They live in bloody Wilsden or somewhere daft like that. But she says she's happy here. Not many white people are left who like West Bowling as much as she does. If she did want to move, she wouldn't even need to put a 'For Sale' sign on, her house would sell no messing around. We like the area and because we have families and need more space, we end up buying the houses. We're the only ones who are left. It's getting like that. White people see that there's a lot of Pakistanis and they get put off. They might think it'll be hard for them to fit in which is daft if you think about it, it's still more their country than it is ours.

If I had to, if I really had to, I could move, but why should I? It's a good area if you know it. That's why people give it a bad name, because they don't know it. To me what's worse is the coppers. I'm not saying everyone around here's an angel and nothing bad goes on. Drug dealers are common compared with other places. You get little bits of this and that but I don't see it as major crime wave stuff. My mates in Heaton, Thornton and up by Odsal, they go on like they have more trouble than we do! Crime's gone down a bit, but not because of the coppers – that started when we got camera-d up. That's had an effect, a good effect. Still gangsters out there and even more wannabes. To me, the drug dealers and the police are the top two bad things. Until you get them sorted out, you won't really see underneath and inside the place.

It's not like a really posh upper-class area, you can see that, but it's not like a project or something daft like that. A lot of my mates, they call it names like 'ghetto', or 'the 'hood' or 'Westside' like it's America, but it's not like that to me. I go along with it but that's just a bit of a joke, is that. No one takes it seriously. It's not that poor, if you think about it. House prices are still going up. For silly money, houses are going. I don't know how people afford it but they do.

I went to Oxford a few months ago and you should have seen it there: *blingers* everywhere you looked! In Bradford, there's a lot of that. Everyone's into money. I mean, I am, too, but not like one hundred and fifty per cent like some of them. I don't wear no rocks or nowt like that. My dad would kill me for a start. I like good clothes, but who doesn't? Odd label here and there isn't going to kill me. Good trainers – comfortable and a bit of something else to them. Normal stuff, I call it.

I can't say I want to move out of West Bowling because I don't. Born and brought up here so it means a lot. You know everyone, everyone knows you and you know the place inside out. To someone else, to someone who hasn't been a part of it, it's just another area. Just houses and streets and people, but to us lot who live here, it's a lot.

Roll A Giro

I used to work on the *M606*. Sitting on your arse putting some screws in boards. All you had to do is get some screws, put them in, connect some wires, stuff like that, nothing major, not hard, just sitting down all day. That job I didn't like. My cousin was the line leader, then below him there was another one we used to be under. He'd tell us, 'Do this, do that blah blah blah.' He didn't really like me. I used to answer back to the guy: 'Why should I do this? Why isn't he doing it?' At the end of the day I still used to do it.

Dad goes, 'Let's open a business up.' Injuries, accidents. Someone was telling me, it's going to finish all this business about injuries. Dad goes, 'No, no, no: do it. Blah blah blah, do it for a few months and see how it goes.' The first few months was proper dead. After that people got to know us, people started coming in. One person with a PI – personal injury – in a week is more than enough. Someone comes to me, 'I've had the accident. This is what happened – someone hit into me, these are the people in my car, this is what I've done so far.' I write it all down. If they need a car I get them a courtesy car. I get an engineer to come down, check your car out, he'll estimate, I'll ring you up. After a few months you put your claim in.

I bought a nice car but now I'm sick of it – *Subaru Impreza*.

I paid six grand. I think it's alright, then I think, 'What am I doing with this car? Car's bullshit, a bad investment. Buy some property, pull off rent. Invest the money. Invest the money.' The car business is alright; if you make a few hundred pounds out of a car you're laughing. Knocking a couple of cars a week, that's asking a lot.

My father, he's into money. He gets up six days a week at his normal time, does his garage, comes back to the shop. If anything needs doing in the shop he'll do it. He's a workaholic, never stops. He comes to the shop, does bits and bats, stacking up, gives a lecture – 'What are you doing here? How come this is expensive, why have you bought this?' As soon as he comes, everyone legs it, because they know he's going to grip everyone. They go to the back, put their head down and start doing something that makes them look busy. He goes home, reads *namaz* and that's about it.

A few mates, about six/seven of us, we used to roll a giro – have a smoke. Go to quiet places, weird places like a forest or a wood, park up, get stoned and have a laugh. One day, me and my mate were just sitting down and somehow Islam just cropped up and he goes, 'Yeah, I've been thinking about it a long time, what we are doing now is not right.' About two years ago we were on Manchester Road. There were a few cassettes in this car and we listened and it started getting to us: what we'd done and what we should be doing, stop this crap and get on the right path. After that I started to read *namaz*, started to read more books.

I've got a kid, he's nearly two now. I want him to be on the right track leaning towards Islam. He can do all this stuff but I'm telling the rules initially – don't do this, don't do that. I went to the mosque when I was a kid. I didn't learn much about Islam at the mosque. That's the problem with these mosques, they never teach you properly. They don't teach you how Islam evolved, the prophet Muhammad – peace be upon him – his life, and stuff like that. They teach you nothing. That is changing. I've seen a few dynamic classes, but before that no mention of anything: just go to your mosque, read, go home and do your normal stuff.

All of us used to live together in these streets: my dad and three brothers. All the family used to live in one house. When we were younger we used to hang around together, do our own little thing, sports, snooker. We never used to get in trouble. Nowadays kids of sixteen/seventeen: chest out, bodies out, big timers walking around the streets, about six or seven of them together. When you look at them, you think, 'Come on, man. Just chill out.' I had mates but they weren't like that. These guys, they have one dog. Let it loose in the park, get a buzz out of that. Idiots. When they see a *gora*. 'You white this, you white that.' Seventeen/eighteen years olds acting big in front of their mates, big time: 'What are you looking at? Are you looking at me? I'll sort you out. I'll do this to you, I'll do that to you.' The *gora*'s there on his own, and he's saying, 'No, no, no, look sorry.' I've seen it a few times on Oak Lane. It calms down but what's going on there?

I moved up near the *BRI*. Nice and quiet. Your own garden, privacy, do what you like. You've got your own drive. You can't leave your car outside in these streets. There's glass from windows getting smashed up, cars getting nicked. The other day there was some guy on Victor Road. His van was on a recovery truck. Overnight someone burned it down.

There's a few takeaways on Oak Lane. My uncle used to work there and he goes, 'It used to be so busy before the riots, it was unbelievable, but now no *gora* goes there, nobody wants to park his car there.' *Gorays*, they've stopped coming to Oak Lane. There are a few who've stuck by, who like it. People who live on estates, in flats, they hate pakis. They think, we live here, we're English and look at these pakis: got nice houses, driving big posh cars. I don't think there are any poor Pakistani people.

The BNP, it's been going on for ages. It was the way they were saying it: 'I want to shoot Muslims. I want to get outside there, I want to get a Transit, machine gun, a million bullets and I want to go outside a mosque and just blow them up.' There's a hill up there, one of them goes: 'You can spot every fucking paki from there. I'll bomb 'em.' I thought, 'Fucking hell, man, in case these lot do get elected, we're out.'

Paper   Cowboys

We knew the BNP were coming, why they were coming down. I still remember the day. It was a Saturday. Australia were playing England and Gilchrist was killing them. I was working up on Rooley Lane, doing the six-two that week, so on the weekend I was knackered.

I came out at about eight o'clock. From where I live you could see the flames and you could see all the smoke going up. I went down where the council houses are, down Whetley Hill, just before White Abbey Road starts. There was this proper clown. I don't know who he was, where he'd come from. For me this was just some idiot. He walks past me, wearing one of those bandanas around his face, over his mouth like a mask, shouting 'Jihad!' That's what he was shouting: 'Jihad!' I just looked at him and I thought I bet you don't even know what that means. A mate of mine, he was really angry about it and he was shouting at all these people, 'You sons of bitches! Why are you calling us Jihadis!?'

There's this pub just across from my house. It's converted into a house now but at the time it was a pub. It was late, Saturday night. We'd seen a curtain flicker in this pub. They'd set fire to it. Me and this other guy from an amusement arcade down the road, we were walking towards the doors of the pub and he says to me, 'You realise that if we get caught in here they're going to do us, they're going to do us clean.' And I just says, 'Look, if someone gets burned in there, then we're going to have to live with that.' So we got in and we went upstairs. There was one room that was on fire but I think the whole place would have caught on pretty soon. There was this door going upstairs and they'd put one of those gambling machines – a one-arm bandit – in front of the door to stop anybody getting out. Now we definitely thought there was somebody in there. So we pushed that machine away. Me and him, we're scared now, as in, 'We've walked into a pub, police could arrive any moment and we'll get arrested.' But luckily for us the local Father – the local Priest, the Vicar – he came in at the same time. When he came in we knew nothing's going to happen to us now. We searched the whole place. Luckily there was no one in there.

The worst thing was that pub on fire. I've seen these *baycharay*, old innocent white people. They were just old white people stood there shaking. Why? What's the point? Why go and sabotage innocent old people? Okay, they got them out of the pub, but what's the point? We spoke to this copper here from Liverpool the next day. He was saying to us, 'All these people are doing is they're messing it up for themselves.' He gives it, 'I was involved in the Liverpool riots in eighty-two/ eighty-three, Toxteth,' and he gives it, 'They're still paying for it now.'

It was violent but there was no protest, there was no focus. There wasn't a cause. It was all about ego, a bunch of lads with nowt better to do. Just idiots throwing stones. Throwing a few stones doesn't make you a man. When you're doing a violent protest it never works anyway. That was the question, 'What are you people rioting against? Are you rioting against racism? Are you rioting against the police? Are you rioting against the government? Immigration? What?' The sad thing is it sticks — mud sticks.

The strongest part about a guy is if he can actually walk away, but I can't. If someone shows me attitude, I've got too much of an ego to back away. I have to shout back, argue, fight back, whatever. If someone throws something at me, I'm going to throw the same back. I've always had a reputation of being a handy guy so I've always had the ego of that as well. *Now* what happens is if you want to fight someone one-on-one, someone's going to pull a gun out. Even if there's no guns, there's ten of them that'll jump you. There's no one-on-one any more. There's too much attitude out there, a lot of paper cowboys. The Asian culture in Bradford, it's just not for me any more. Bradford, born and brought up. That's all I've grown up with. I didn't mind it until recently.

It's sad, it upsets me, but the only time I come in contact or communicate with white people is when I'm working, when I do my regular forays into call centre work. That's the only time. At a personal level my experiences are only with Asian people. I've grown up with them, so I'm not going to deviate from them, but, our social activities, what we do are totally different. I don't like to sit around and have a smoke, because I don't smoke. I don't like to sit around and have a drink, because I don't drink. I do sit on the street because that's where I've been brought up. I like it sometimes, when it's a sunny day and I've

91

got my little drink in my hand there and I'm just sitting around at the end of my garden, summat to eat, chilling out.

People just like to sit in the street – selling drugs, relaxing, smoking drugs. Lads sit around and talk about stuff – 'Do you see that bad boy driving this, he's driving that, or he's got a bad car, he's got this, he's got that.' You just think, 'There's more to life than this.' Not my idea of a full life. Okay I might not be earning thirty grand a year at the moment. I'm now twenty-three, but at least I'm trying to do something that's a bit more constructive and at least it fulfils me.

I see people driving flash cars. It's like, 'Well I know where you live and I know what you do.' I feel sorry for them. When you're older and you're more independent it becomes present. It's quite freaky to see what actually goes on out there. In order for a person to make money, they have to be selling certain things. I've got little cousins round here. There are crowds, all this gang culture, gun culture, drug culture. But I can't keep an eye on these little ones. I really don't know what they're doing. I do try to chase them around, but they're at an impressionable age. We're brought up to be Muslims and if you think about it, in the long run none of this is going to help you. Okay, I'm not the best Muslim, I don't read *namaz*, I just read *Jumma* some of the time. I'm not going to lie, I do mess around with girls but things like making a fast buck and stuff, it's just not for me.

I'd like to be in Bradford in ten years, but the way it's going, I doubt it. From what I've heard, Birmingham's pretty similar. Manchester, that's pretty much similar. There's too much of a gun culture – this Afro-American kind of influence. What we see on TV about this gun culture going on over there, we're bringing it over here – *Boyz 'n the Hood, Menace II Society*. It's all about people who have no direction. With the generation older than me, they have a lot more thought for their parents than we do. People who are older than us think about their parents but that kind of thing is evaporating now.

No Salaams

On this programme – *Calendar News* – there's this *buddee*, coming out with it, 'Oh, you can't walk into some areas.' That's a load of crap. There's loads of white people working in our area; they never get grief, they never get trouble. Those 'no go' areas, it's just crap. One white guy probably got beat up for probably coming out with something stupid, or said summat wrong to someone, and that's it. One *goree* on there lives in our area, she buys stuff from *aapnay*, she's mingling with *aapnay* all the time, and then she's got the cheek to say all this stuff about *aapnay*: they're like this and they're like that. That's politics, that's what it comes down to. Good news – bad news obviously for us.

When it comes to us going into a white area in Keighley, we don't have to say nothing and we get grief. We just don't do it. Taxi drivers get grief, never mind us. About three or four year ago my mate were in a school. It's mainly white populated. My mate, he's a big lad for his age, he goes, 'There's going to be a kick-up after school. *Gorays* are after us and they're going to beat us up later on.' Coppers got to hear there was going to be a kick up with Asians and *gorays*, so they must have been on guard an' all. We didn't have a clue what was going on. We just parked up and next we see these *aapnay* legging it from the park. We were standing outside the car, just having a laugh and that, and next thing you know, all we saw was about twenty/ thirty *goray*. Balaclavas, baseball bats, legging towards us. We all jumped back in the car – a shabby *XR2*. The *goray* were just about to get to us. I still remember it to this day. My cousin who was driving, he just pulled out, he didn't even have any spin off because it wasn't even an *XR2* – it was just a normal 1.2 or summat; an *XR2* look-alike. So he pulled out, went round this taxi parked in the middle of the road picking up a fare – guess what's coming up in front of us? Cop car! He seen us pull out like that, and go. What did that copper do? Turn around, started chasing *us*! My mate, he panicked, didn't stop, went down a street, come round a corner, and then guess what? Coppers. We were surrounded.

This is how bad his car was: the door was hung on by sellotape, hammered on with bits of wood. Copper goes, 'What are they?'

My mate goes, 'That's part of the door, officer.'

Copper goes, 'They look like weapons to me.'

Laughing our heads off, but we go, 'What we done wrong? Didn't you see them white lads with balaclavas on, with baseball bats coming toward us? That's the only reason we went that fast.'

He got done, obviously. Got banned.

Coppers in Keighley are no good. Generally, I don't think they're straight up. Bradford coppers are not as bad as Keighley, Skipton and Colne. They are three places I know for a fact are no good. The young ones that have come in now, they're alright because they understand. The older coppers they just keep stopping *aapnay*, the usual crap. Stop you for nothing.

Ten years ago my brother used to have this white Corolla XE coupé and he used to go to Burnley every day. He used to have to go through Colne and he got pulled every friggin' day. It got to one stage, he got pulled four times: routine check. Routine check!

I've got three points. On New Year's Day, I got them. It was about four in the morning, I was coming back from Bradford, God knows where we went. A guy *gunned* me. Fair enough. After that I've never been caught for speeding or 'owt like that, never done it – learned my lesson. I don't want any more points, full-stop. But I've been fined for silly stuff. Like *plates* for example. The plates were on my car already. It's not as if you can't read them. I've seen ridiculous plates on the road, and I mean ridiculous number plates. The copper, he stopped me, and I goes, 'I'm sorry, officer, they come with the car. I'm sorry I didn't know they were illegal. I've been driving this car for over six months and I've never been stopped once about my plates.' They were a bit smaller than the normal size, but you could read them clearly. He was just one of them, you could tell just by looking at him. He had a new apprentice, a *goree*, sat in the passenger side. I sat with him and that and he goes, 'Oh, sorry I'm going to have to fine you.'

I go, 'Officer, what's the normal thing you do? You normally give a person a warning, don't you, first? You tell them to get them changed. If I knew, I wouldn't have had them on my car. I've even been pulled and the coppers have never mentioned my plates before.' That copper, he fined me, the bastard.

I was coming back from Bradford; picked up some blinds for my house. They worked out thirty pounds cheaper from

Bradford. I picked them up after work. I thought, man, I've saved thirty pounds – sorted. Coming back, Manningham Park, that bus lane. Going along, loads of traffic in the right hand lane. Most of the time the traffic on that side is usually taking a right towards Canal Road. I was in the right lane first, then I thought, 'Oh, bugger this! I'm not waiting here.' Lots of people were turning right, so I went in the bus lane, just for ten seconds. I looked up ahead: shit! A few coppers parked up just before the lights. They weren't exactly parked up, they were standing with cameras. So I just pulled out into the bus lane then I went back.

I was in my GSI, a sporty car. I was going along, and the next thing you know this *aapna* copper comes out of nowhere, jumps in the middle of the road: 'Stop!'

Pulls me over. Cool bastard, the way he did it. He looked at me and he goes, 'Right!' And he goes over to his other younger copper mate. You could tell he was a new lad an' all, didn't have a clue what's going on. He goes, 'Book him.'

'What the fuck? What for?'

He goes, 'You know why, we've got you on camera.'

I go, 'For God's sake, officer. I thought the traffic was taking a right.'

He goes, 'Well, we're doing a clamp down on people using the bus lane.'

I go, 'Well, I didn't exactly *use* the bus lane, did I?'

He goes, 'Well, I'm sorry, mate: you're taking a fine.'

I got a thirty pound fine! A bit pointless that journey to Bradford.

There is a difference between Keighley and Bradford in the *aapnay* attitudes. For example, when you go to Bradford, us lot, we see someone we know, we shake hands: *Asalamoalaikum-Walaikumsalaam*. Respect and everything. When *aapnay* come from out of town to Keighley and that, they don't get no *Salaams*, no nothing. I've got a lot of mates in Bradford and it's probably different, their way of thinking. It's maybe because all the time, they're *aapnay* full-stop. In Bradford they're always *aapnay* – 24-7.

My brothers have moved from Keighley. I'm not really happy where I am. I've lived here all my life now so I've got to that stage where I need a change. But I don't know, I'm not too fussed. We've got two houses, eight bedrooms. We've got a massive house. All I've got is me, my wife, my son and my mum and dad. I'm thinking, if I sell them two houses what am I going to get for them? Property prices in our area are shit; everywhere else they're good. They do get sold straight away but only *aapnay* buy them. They're touching forty/forty-five thousand pounds for a four bedroom house. That's nothing. Nowadays you can get a one bedroom house for forty-five thousand pounds. I'm thinking eighty grand for both houses, being realistic. My mum and dad don't want to move, full-stop. If I sell my house and get forty-five grand, what am I going to buy? I don't want a one bedroom house or two bedroom house. It's not enough. I'm going to wait a while, wait until the prices crash.

I've been working over five years in the Tax Office, and I've got to that stage where I'm fed up of it now. The job I started with in the Tax Office I loved to bits. Tracing people, like detective work. I'm really handy with computers, really quick. We used to have a list of people that had moved address, so we'd go looking on the computer to get it. Phoning their previous employers, phoning their agents, phoning the house. That's a job I enjoyed. You'd go around hunting them on the computer. I used to find them nine out of ten times; I was the best in the business at that game.

I got moved. That's the bad thing about Inland Revenue. They move you when they feel like it. When there's work demand somewhere else, they move you. I'd been in that Tracing Unit over three years and they thought, right, he's experienced, we'll get him doing summat else. They got me doing bloody checks in the Banking Unit. I was stuck there for a year and I hated it. Easy work, really easy work. So I thought, 'Sod this, I'll ask for a move.' But they don't always move you to where you want. The places you don't put, you get them. That's what happened to me! I put, 'I want to move back to Tracing.'

They go, 'No, you can't move back to Tracing because you've been there already.'

So I got moved to this other place – Network – I've been there like three months now and I'm fed up. It's mainly paperwork. Just routine stuff, everyday stuff. It's crap, it's boring and I'm fed up. I'm thinking of looking along the lines of like council related jobs, because they pay well. Council, well, they pay better than bloody Inland Revenue.

Snookered

We used to do mischief. Mischief Night was a night when you were excused to do whatever you wanted to do. You'd know: don't get carried away but you were licensed to do summat silly. And what we'd do is we'd put a bottle on somebody's door handle, knock on it and when they opened, the bottle comes down and smashes. If it was snowing, pelting snowballs and that at buses. Once, this guy come running out of the bus and he started chasing me. He was maybe in his early forties or summat, and I was about nine or ten years old. I ran into my snicket and I went into an outside toilet and locked it. My dad come out and says, 'What's going on?'

'This lad's been throwing snowballs at buses.'

My dad went to the door and asked who was in there and I said, 'It's me.'

I opened the door. My dad started kicking the shit out of me. The man said, 'It's alright, leave him alone now. It was only a snowball!'

My parents kept me out of a lot of trouble. That was the understanding they had with their children. Nowadays it's different. If my kids swear, the only punishment I give them is make them stand in a corner and face the wall, take some of their liberties away.

Nowadays, fireworks in letterboxes, slashing car tyres, you

name it. In them days, coppers used to walk up and down. In a day you'd probably see about four or five different bobbies on the beat. The law, you were afraid of it in them days. Nowadays, nobody's scared of 'owt. There's nowt to put them off from doing anything. You nick a car and end up in a police station interview, and they let you back out again in two or three hours and you're on your way. Attend police bail, come down a month later, get done for clocking a car, get a little fine or maybe a few hours community service.

I liked school, but not the fact that you used to get educated at school. A laugh, get out of the house, because there's more rules at home than school. I did go to the mosque until I was fourteen. My kids don't go to a mosque, they go to a *madrassah*. They believe in Islam, they treat Islam with love; there's nowt forced. They tell them values, how to respect your elders; this is good, this is bad, this is how you do this. They tell them all the ways of life as well. In our case it wasn't like that. Go in with your hat, a *Qur'an* in your hand or whatever. Didn't have a clue what it meant. It's a lot of progress.

My parents, when they come over here it wasn't just my father what came here. My father's brother came here, his cousins came here, and his relatives, and all his village turned up at just about the same time. When they do that they bring everything with them; they've still got all their culture from over there. Us Pakistanis, we're compressed. They've come in a group, everybody can communicate, they don't have to change much.

In them days the cheapest kind of houses to buy were back-to-back and terraced. When our dads came over they were working not even to save but to send back home to the rest of their family. They didn't give a shit about their kids. Their job is just to feed them, make sure they grow up and get married and away. They'd wake up, have summat to eat, get the *roti* in them little tins, get to work. Fourteen/fifteen hours later come back home, have summat to eat, straight to bed. If there were eight days a week, they would probably do eight days. Parents didn't have much time. Our fathers, when they initially came over here, they said, 'We're just going to make our bit of money and we're going back.'

My mum come over in the late sixties and at that time people used to share houses. My dad used to share with his cousins and his brothers and my mum used to have to cook and wash for all of them. I come from a big family – two brothers and four sisters. There were four of us stuck into one little room and there were three of us stuck into another little room. Now it's completely different. We've a lot more understanding, we talk to kids. In them days if summat happened between parents or whatever, it was nothing to do with kids. Nowadays you try to explain to your kids what's going on with the adults.

I got snookered into marriage. Forced marriage, really. Twelve years now. I was a naughty boy. I wouldn't call myself a bad lad – sneaking out at night time, and just hanging about, not doing my school work properly and stuff like that. My older sister, she's about eight/nine years older than me, she got married back home in Pakistan. She was born here, went over there and got married, came back over here and he was still there. They didn't get on, the family fell out. It didn't work out so she got divorced and had to get married again. An older woman to get married in them days was a bit difficult. Especially somebody who's been divorced. So my sister got married to this guy on the condition that I was going to marry his sister.

My dad says, 'We're going to go back to Pakistan. Your sister's getting married, your mum's going over. I'm taking your little sister, you come over, as well.'

I says, 'I'll tell you what, I don't want to go over.'

He says, 'No, no please. It's your sister's wedding.'

My older brother, he was in a job, so he couldn't go, and the younger one was still in school. I was unemployed. My dad says, 'Come on, I'll take you over.'

So we went. They started arranging wedding things. When you're a teenager you know what the crack is – you know why you're going to go to Pakistan. I said to my parents, 'If you take me to Pakistan don't think I'm going to get married.'

And my mum went, 'You shouldn't be getting married.'

I said to my dad, 'Look, I'm not going to go back home. Don't expect me getting married.'

And he says, 'No, no, Son. Don't worry about getting married.'

I didn't believe my dad but I trust my mum. So I went back home. They started doing wedding arrangements for my sister and maybe two weeks into it my dad sits me down and says, 'Oh, look, you're in Pakistan anyway…this is a good family, this is this and this is that.'

I knew what was coming. My dad sat me down and said, 'Oh, I'm going to get you married. What do you think about it?'

I said, 'No Dad, I'm not getting married.'

He started explaining to me, 'This is good for us. We're going to grow old and they're going to look after us, they'll look after you. Your sister's getting married here and there will be some kind of protection for your sister.'

I says, 'No, no.'

My dad sort of fell out with me, told my mum to have a word. He could threaten me but I'd been there before. I was wise about it. Everybody who went to Pakistan were coming back married men. I knew you could get a lift to the British Embassy and they'd get you on the next flight back within a couple of days. My mum sat me down and said, 'Look, you might as well get married here.'

I said, 'Look, Mum, I told you before I come, I don't want to get married here.'

And my mum said, 'Your dad's going to be upset.'

She started telling me the advantages of it. I said, 'Alright, Mum. Just leave it with me and let me think about it.'

About a week on they are doing my wedding arrangements and I've not even said yes to a marriage. So I grabbed my *maamoo*. My *maamoo* is only about three or four years older than me. I said, 'Look I'm a bit stuck here. They're trying to get me married off. I don't want to get married off. You have a chat with my mum.'

He says, 'I can't, your mum isn't going to listen to me.'

I said to him, 'Tell you what, sort me out a lift. I've got money on me, get me to the British Embassy. I'm going to fly back, man.'

He sat me down and he says, 'She's a good girl, she isn't

going to live with this lot any more. She will be over there with you.'

They pushed me into a corner. There was nobody on my side, and when you're by yourself you've no choice.

I wasn't interested in it. My intention was to do *nikkah* there, come back over here and finish it. If my dad kicked me out of the house I could carry on with my life. I was eighteen/nineteen, I was streetwise so it wasn't a problem for me.

I come back. For maybe a year and a half I didn't write to her, I didn't talk to her; nothing. She used to write me letters. There wasn't much in them. I didn't write back. My sister used to write a letter back on my behalf now and then. When we got married I talked to her once or twice. My mate since school, he's a bit wiser than me – only just got married recently – he gives it to me, 'You've got married, bring her over. This is no good. If you have to, have a bird, and just carry on, but don't ruin her life.'

So I took his advice. I'd take advice off a pisshead, me. There are certain things in life that happen because they have to happen. And I thought that because marriage has happened it's summat that you have to do now. You have to act like a married man, even though there was no love involved.

I brought her over and tried to make a go of it. I wouldn't say those married years were good years. You enjoy it when you have your first child. I had problems with my wife for the last two or three years. She's got family. She's got that brother that married my sister, and she's got a *maamoo* here. She didn't want to live with my family in my house. So I says to her, 'If you want to move out you can move out.'

She says, 'Yeah, I'll move out.'

I said, 'Alright, go ahead then, pack your bags and I'll take you wherever you want to go.'

She went to her uncle's house two hundred yard up the road. She's a good person, but it's not the person I wanted to marry. We're different people, different to what they are, completely. When I say 'we' I'm on about us British Pakistanis compared to them original Pakistanis. Completely different people we are. We take the good from our culture, and we take the good from this English culture. Humanity, is that what you call it, there's a lot of *insaaneeyat* in English people. Put it this way, a Pakistani who lives in Pakistan has got more rights in this country than he has in his own country. It's a very poor country. With there not being that many well paid jobs, you've got to be bent, corrupt.

I've been to Pakistan three or four times. The first time, I went when my sister got married. The second time, I enjoyed myself. I went because my mates went and we had a right laugh. That time we went just for a doss around. I was only home for about two or three days. For about six weeks, I had the time of my life. Following that I went because my dad wanted to build some houses, for whenever he goes. He can't go no more, he's poorly now. The houses, they're just there. No nothing, just locked up. They're not even fully completed yet. Going to Pakistan is like going to visit family. Never mind visiting family there, I don't like visiting family here. If you come from a big family, people are buzzing around you. If you went to Europe, nobody knows who you are, you do whatever you want to do, you can be yourself, nobody's interested in you. Friends, I don't mind, because they're neutral. Family friends are a lot better than relatives.

Back home, when a son is born they say, 'My child is going to go to England.' Get on a plane and come over here, and they try to live their lives. Back home *mangaythurs* don't work. When they have to go and clean chicken's arses out at a poultry farm they think, 'This isn't what we were promised. Money growing on trees, and honey flowing out of taps and stuff. I didn't know this was going to happen!' They think these streets are paved with gold. And here it's not like that. You work hard for your money, it's hard graft. Maybe after ten years they get to appreciate the fact – it's not easy living here. I've known *mangaythurs* that have been here for over ten years. When they go back, even *mangaythurs* have problems living over there, because they've picked up from us.

I'll let my kids choose where they want to get married. Obviously, Muslims. If they wanted me to choose for them I'd probably get them a few options here and there. But if they choose on their own, no problem to me. Life is to do with communicating – you've got to talk, have a relationship. My wife's not exactly talking a different language. She's been here ten or twelve years, I've adjusted to try and communicate with her, and she's adjusted, but it's hard work.

I love my kids and I miss my kids. I sent a couple of letters saying I'm wanting to see them but they said, 'No we're not going to let you see the kids.' I had to go through the courts. I put one of those applications in for my kids not to leave the country. I don't want them to go over there. At the end of the day, who would go for me to Pakistan to try to do peace talks

112

with them? You've more chance of resolving matters over here than going over there. So I put an application in to see my kids. She don't phone me, I don't phone her. There's no other way of doing it.

I live in Marshfields, Little Horton ward. West Bowling is on the other side of the road. The neighbourhood round here is brilliant for us who live here. This is my home, I'd struggle to move out of here. I've got a takeaway next door to me, on the other side I've got a newsagents, I've got a chip shop, a video shop, a butcher's round the corner, Morrisons five minutes up the road. We run off each other. I buy chicken and chips off a Pakistani, I go and get my hair cut from an Asian guy – he relies on me. I've got a mosque one hundred yards there, and another one a hundred yards in front of me – you can't go wrong. All the family, all friends and everything, you don't even have to be home and you know your house is safe with everybody around you. When we moved in here, I think there was only about two or three Pakistanis around in this area. Now probably there's only about two or three *goray* left. I'm talking over five hundred houses now. People get better off, they try to move out or try to have a change.

I've been a private hire driver on and off twelve/thirteen years. It's a lazy job. Once you get into it, it's very hard for you to do anything else. Not a job I'd recommend if you've got a social life – too many hours in a week. When I first started – I was single, no kids – I used to put in up to fifteen/sixteen hours a day. When you've worked fifteen/sixteen hours, you can earn a decent wage, summat that you can live off. But once you get married it's a completely different story. You've got to spread your time around. You work six days, you have a day off to do the shopping, doctor's appointments. You squeeze it all into one day, and your day off's wasted.

I wouldn't call it enjoyable. It's summat you have to do. Pissheads come into it on the evening work, after ten o'clock. You get used to it. It happens that many times, you accept it as being normal. They can't help it – they're pissed, and they talk shit. It's the same person you pick up during the day and they're sound as a pound. It's not just *gorays* that get funny when they're pissed, *aapnay* when they're pissed, they're worse. They 'brother this' and 'brother that', but they're full of shit. When I first used to do it and somebody got funny, it used to make my blood boil. You wanted to fight every job. But you understand they're a different person during the day

The best thing about taxiing is there is money in your pocket. You're not waiting 'til the end of weekend or month. End of your shift, whatever you've got is in your pocket. When you put a good week in there's five hundred pounds in your pocket – twenty-five thousand pounds a year, what solicitors get. I used to have my own firm for about eight or nine months. You have to show authority, disagree with people, and I don't like that, not my game. I'm not a boss, it's not in my nature.

Beenie

My grandad punched a horse once, knocked it out. He had an older brother who was a bit of a player, a bit of a poser. It's like these days people with their BMs, he had his horse. My grandad was much more of a working class guy; making sure his house, the crops were okay. So one day his brother's horse was eating the crops, eating whatever was being grown. My grandad went to his brother and said, 'Big brother. The horse, don't let it loose like that because it ruins all the crop.'

My grandad, he had a really short temper. I don't know how he managed to keep cool with his brother about this, but he said, 'I spend hours on this crop and your horse just takes minutes and it's gone. If it does it again, right, you'll know about it.'

And his older brother says, 'Forget about it. It's only a horse. What's the big deal? What are you doing, why are you making a fuss about vegetables and a horse?'

So the next time it happened, my grandad went up to it and cracked it one. Killed it, with one knock, honest to God. He grabbed a hold of the horse and pulled it to his brother's house and said, 'Here, here's your horse.'

My grandad and my uncles, they're into traditional Pakistani sports – *Kabadi*, *Beenie*. My grandad did *Beenie* and my uncle did it as well. My grandad was a champion about fifty years ago.

My dad he's not too big, so he could never do it. My dad wanted one of us to continue but I was working and wasn't really into this. When I started weight training, being a bit more fitness conscious, my dad put me into the sport.

There's a lot about technique and training, not just strength. When I lost the first time around, I didn't know anything. I didn't have the timing. It's like when you kick a football it's not all about power, it's timing. You have to be very strategic, it's about how clever you are in this game. When they fall down they're wasting time, they're conning the referee. And because it's a timed sport, wasting time's important. So you go down, you get up, and you go down again. Time's ticking away. There's a person who taught me a couple of things. He's twenty-seven; nobody wants to hold with him. He's clean, no dirt involved, doesn't cheat. He will rip you if you do it clean. The only time he's lost is 19-20 – one point in it – and the guy who beat him doesn't want a rematch. That should tell you something. He said to me, 'When somebody's holding your arm, you bring it down when *you* want to. When you think it's the right time to hit the shot, when all your body and all your mind is ready, go for it then.'

After every tournament for about a week I'm really tired. When you make your entrance, it's like when boxers come into the arena for a fight. A lot of guys jump up and down and make noises and all that. I did that a couple of times and noticed it saps your energy. Everybody's smoking, it's very warm, you're sweating – it's like being in Brazil. The last thing you need to be doing is losing that energy by jumping up and down like an idiot. You're only doing it for like a minute's time, but it takes a lot of energy out of you. The last tournament I did I didn't do any of that jumping around, and people were thinking I was scared – not moving around because he's nervous. I knew why I wasn't moving around – I was saving my energy and it paid off.

I remember talking to this solicitor once. He said, 'What do you classify yourself as? Think about this carefully. Tell me what you think you are. Are you British? Are you Pakistani? Are you British Muslim? What are you? Are you somebody who doesn't want nothing to do with Britain?'

I didn't really think about it. 'There's two things here,' I said. 'I was born and bred in this country, I've lived here all my life. Where you're born, that's the country you grow to like. I've also been going to Pakistan to study my roots and where I'm from. If I was to live in Pakistan for eight months I'd miss England, because this is what I've known. This is my country. But you can't forget your roots. That's where my parents are from, that's where my background is.'

So this guy, the solicitor, he turns round and says to me, 'Yeah, but how long will that last?'

I said, 'I can't guarantee anything. That's not in my hands.'

It's up to the parents. I've got three kids and I wouldn't want them to forget their roots. They are born in this country and this is their country, there's no doubt about that. I'd say you're still a Pakistani. It's the roots, it's part of your heritage, it's part of what you are. You should not forget what you are and who you are. When you miss those lines, that's when you don't know.

That One Gora

Our parents man, stories they tell us. One day my dad and this other guy, they let it slip that they were fighting. I went, 'Hang on, fighting?' He goes, 'All the time. We used to go to the cinema and *goray* would start on us. You have to stick up for your friend. You're not friends, you're brothers. Without each other you have nothing.'

My dad's seventy-odd now, he came here when he was in his teens. Settled down then brought my mum over. My big brother was born, my sister and I was born. Then we had to sell the house because back home something happened and they needed money. So my dad had to sell the house and we moved in with people. To this day them people we regard as family – how many people would rock somebody else's child to sleep when you've got four kids of your own? Dad come back, started all over again, scrimping, saving, and then we finally managed to get a house of us own.

My dad worked very hard, all our parents did back then – twelve hour shifts, seven 'til seven. He worked in textiles. How many of our parents did not do textiles when they come over here? We've got it easy now. Our kids have got grandparents but when we were born our grandparents were thousands of miles away. I can remember my dad going to work in a morning. He used to come home at seven, shaving downstairs

– splashing on the Old Spice, help my mum dress us, wash us, feed us, take us to school and then get up and bring us back from school, take us to mosque, bring us back, and then go to work. Five days a week.

There were a few businesses they were looking at and they settled on this corner shop. It was round the corner from where we used to live, so there was no big upheaval. All the schools were the same, all the neighbours the same and everything. We did *daar*, borrowed so much money off mates, owed so many people. My dad pulled a partition down, made the shop bigger. Did so much to the building when we first got it. My dad goes, 'Right, Monday to Thursday eight 'til ten, Friday eight 'til eleven, Saturday eight 'til eleven and Sunday nine 'til ten.' The first three or four years we were paying people back mad-style.

Now, my father and sister run it. It used to be an off-licence, sell alcohol like nobody's business. Sometimes used to take two or three trips to the cash and carry every day. Used to make some mad money. We used to have a lot of white customers when we bought it twenty-odd years ago. There were mini scuffles. *Goray* would come in:

'Oh, it's cheaper in Morrisons.'

'Well why don't you go to Morrisons?'

'Because it's shut. It's half past ten.'

'Yeah, fella. You've got half an hour and we're going to shut then. Make your mind up.'

About a year into the shop, Saturday evening, there were about thirty to forty *goray* outside going, 'You black bastards.'

Bricks were flying. Every window put through. Straight away you saw what they were going to do. I was ten years old. I said, 'Right Mum, get all the people in the cellar.'

We didn't have a clue what anybody wanted. I locked my mum in the cellar and I must have rung the police fifteen, twenty times. 'We're coming, we're coming.'

Ten minutes later, 'You said you're coming. They're kicking shit out of my dad out there. What the fuck are you doing?'

They were chucking bricks and we were picking them up and chucking them back. This guy was going to hit my dad. There was one of my dad's mates, this *Imam*, that come to our house. He was about sixty years old, his *daaree* were out there. He grabbed hold of my dad and moved him out of the way. Took a bar to his head. Deaf in one ear.

The police all came and they scarpered. The coppers go, 'Yeah, we got them all and we made charges' and all this. I never heard anything. I know I was a ten-year-old kid but I wanted to know what they got.

We used to do self-service, they were all locals, all of them were fine. Rather than farting around, we used to say, 'Come round and pick up what you want,' and they would just queue up and take it away. I was twelve or thirteen. My dad was getting the attic built and he said to me, 'We'll be back in two minutes.'

My eldest sister was sat in the shop with me. They'd not even been gone up ten seconds and this guy walked in, got behind the counter. I turned around to talk to my sister. This arm come round, I got a knife to my neck.

'Take my money, take my money!'

The next thing you know he's got hold of you by the throat. I still thought he was joking, thinking, 'Bloody hell! This isn't moving.'

I felt it on my neck and I says to my sister, 'Give him whatever he wants and we'll grab him when he gets outside.'

Got out and he started running. As I was chasing him, I was screaming at people, 'Grab him! He's just robbed us!' They moved out of the way.

About six years ago, I went to Glastonbury. We were talking, sat around the camp fire getting stoned and all that. Things come out. They goes, 'What's the worst experience you've had?'

I goes, 'Well, I've had a knife at my neck,' and I goes, 'I watched all these white guys kick fuck out of my dad.'

This *goree* went sour faced, she goes, 'Don't slap me but I was there that night.'

I says to her, 'Look now, I've no ill feelings towards that because that was a long, long time ago. But could you please tell me one thing: what started it? We got battered badly, lucky that we ain't scarred.'

I could walk around like some of my friends, 'white bastards, white bastards' but that doesn't gain anything. This girl, she goes, 'Look, it was alcohol they was after; they were pissed out of their heads. Nobody could stop them doing it.'

When I was a kid it was good because all my friends were here, but people evolve, they move. You see things and you think, 'That's good. I could aspire to have something like that.' Anybody who has an ounce of sense has moved out. We need a bigger house, we need to shut down the shop because it's not running right; just put us out of this misery and move on and just have a normal life where you don't have to walk through a shop to get into your living room. I wouldn't mind that for a change. You've got drug dealers flying up and down streets at two or three o'clock in the morning. Then you've got people coming down on pills, got the music on at six o'clock in the morning. I don't give a monkey's chuff! I've been banging on doors saying, 'Get out or I'll break his legs! I've got nieces and nephews in my house. I'm going to drag you in my house and you're going to rock them to sleep because I aren't doing it!'

My best mate was the second to last white guy to move out. My earliest memories are with him. First mate I made at school. Whenever I go to his house it's like I'm his little brother, whenever he comes to my house, it's like he's my dad's son. When he was a kid and used to get pissed he used to come knocking on our door. Nobody drinks coffee in our house, but my dad used to keep a jar to sober him up. There's been a lot of positives for him living where he's lived all his life. Before he moved out he had his parents living next door to him, so he said, 'Right, I'm going to get a house with a granny flat for them: I want my parents to come with me.'

People say that's because he hung around with Pakistanis a lot. When Pakistanis move, we take our parents – *goray* take them to a nursing home. They didn't want to move. It was simply because the area had gone down the pan. He goes, 'I've only moved because the people that have moved in can't keep the street clean.' The area's a tip and that's why they won't spend money on it. I says to my dad, 'We have to move. This is doing my head in.' People fly up and down them streets, up and down there seventy/eighty miles per hour. Drug dealers – what's two/three grand to them in a car? That's why I can't live there any more.

It's a sign of the times. Did we have *MTV Raps*, did we have ninety-two channels on television? For starters we had no hip hop. I'm not blaming hip hop, I'm blaming mindless kids that watch it and think, 'Well I've not got a character and I've not got an identity of my own, so what I will do is I will take that.' When we were growing up as kids we just went out and played as kids. These guys watch TV and they see it and they think, 'We should be doing that,' not what you should be doing as a kid, which is having fun. We kicked the ball and chased it and it was called football. We played hide-and-seek, we played tig. We had a black and white TV – took twenty minutes to push the button in. Our parents back then would say, *'Aapnee zabaan bolo'*. My parents still say that to me now.

Kids have nowhere to go. We used to have a massive park – they've built over it. Kids in the street, who do they look up to? They look up to people driving past in flash cars who pull up and say, 'Alright how you doin'?' He's only saying 'Alright how you doin'?' because he might know your uncle or your brother. Six months or six years down the line, you'll be dealing for him. I've seen it happen with my own eyes. Their mate is doing it, he's got money, he's got a pager, he's got a telephone, probably going to give him a six hundred pound car. He's going to get a chain, he's going to look hard with it, a gold tooth put in, he's going to get all his hair trimmed off. Kids aspire to be drug dealers. I've seen kids at youth clubs, good kids, and now three or four are dead, and the others are dealing. All of them at some point were best mates but are now trying to kill each other. It's the money, the cash. Got a brand new *Impreza* parked outside the house. All of a sudden you move to a detached house. Parents are accepting it.

If I was to move I'd move to Howarth. I know it's a predominantly white area but you've got moors, you've got greenery, you've got beautiful landscapes. Just lose yourself. It's a lovely place. If you took kids for a walk you'd be taking them for a walk, not to the top or bottom of the street and wait for a car to go past at one hundred miles per hour and then cross the road. An actual normal upbringing where they aren't looking up to people wearing gold chains. That is what I would want to get away from for my nephews, because I can see that on a day-by-day basis they're getting more and more sucked in. I can see it. Their language has changed, the way they speak, *mudda, mudda* is coming out of them.

They're going to predominantly Asian schools, we were going to predominantly white schools. First School it were alright. You go to Middle School, the kids your age were alright, it was the ones three years older in the final year, they were ready to pop – 'black bastards' and all this. When we got to that school the Pakistanis that used to sort things out were leaving, so these young *goray* thought 'Now's our chance'. We were fresh meat, so they came after us. First two years were very hard. The final two years you've just sorted it out and everything was sweet because now the third and fourth years had black and white mates – they'd been at school three years together. When all the big ones disappeared, them few white ones that were left were now the minority and they were like quits. When you got to your Grammar-Upper School: pakis not allowed in tennis courts. Not again! It pisses me off now because I will see loads of Pakistanis ganging up on one or two *goray*. I can't stomach it because I've been that one *gora* or one Pakistani. I've had six or seven *goray* on me, I've been left in woods, had shit kicked out of me.

We play football for these *gora* teams. You've got to socialise with people to get to know them to realise how they play football. For us to succeed we've to be men-of-the-match material every game. We might be a minority, but as a force we're a majority. I want these people to know we're Pakistani. We can run, some of us can fight and eff and blind, some of us are cultured, educated people who deserve equal status. I kid you not, these people were talking to us about arranged marriages, saying, 'Look what is the problem with you people?' We were giving them more feedback than what they were getting from papers.

I don't have a lot of respect for lads in Bradford. If you go anywhere and say you're from Keighley, they laugh at you. When you go to football tournaments and you come up against a team from Bradford you know for a fact that if you start with one you're going to have three hundred coming down. I stay away, I don't have 'owt to do with it. I can't do with the tracky bottoms with Rockport shoes.

Packed Lunch

We used to go to Green Lane First School. Our dad used to give us dinner money. We couldn't do anything with the money other than buy the dinner or maybe buy some bubblies. Our older brother, he was ten or twelve at the time. Because he was a bit older than us, he had different uses for money. So what he used to do was take our dinner money – me and my other brother's – and make us *prantay* at home: pack them up and then send us off to school. But every now and then he'd get the money but he'd forget to make us our food. You'd get to the fourth day or something and he'd say, 'Oh, I forgot', or 'I can't be arsed waking up to make you this food.'

I remember clearly, me and my brother sat there on the bench in the dinner hall with those who had packed lunches. Sat at these big long tables but we'd be turned around, facing the wall. And because it was dinner time, it wasn't like you could go out and play. If you didn't have any dinner you'd all have to be in the dinner hall. Those who had already eaten would be sat in one part of the hall, those who were eating would be sat in another part of the hall. Everyone who was eating their dinner was eating their dinner, and the ones with the packed lunch were eating their packed lunch, and then there was me and my brother sat on this bench. Me and my brother just sat there facing the wall, about two hundred kids eating at the back behind us. We had no food, we had nothing to eat because our big brother took our dinner money and forgot to make us – or couldn't be arsed making us – *prantay*. You're sat there, you're young – five, six or seven – just sat there hungry. We can't look back, we just can't look back, because everyone's eating food and we haven't got no food. And to look back it would be weird because if you looked back you'd see all that food and everybody would be eating. Everybody would be happy and we wouldn't.

Cabbing

I look at all these builders, all these electricians, every one's a cowboy: don't invest anything. They don't even buy their own screwdrivers! If you bought all the proper equipment, all the proper cutting edge gear, you could clock out jobs in no time. You never see them come to your house with a nail-gun – still a nail and a hammer, banging away like that. And you think, spend a few hundred, spend a few grand. There's so much technology that'll make your life easier. Nothing's hard. You put your mind to it you can do anything.

Plumbing, electrician-ing – six month courses, or maybe a year course. Three months of practical, of blowing up someone's house, and that's it, become an electrician. You only need to know household stuff, household electrics. You don't need to know how to build a circuit board, the theory of it.

Cabbing's something easy, something that you can do. It's too easy for me not to do it. I want to do something else but then I think, 'There's nothing that I can do.' Taxiing to me – easy money. If somebody says to me, 'What are you doing these days?' And I say, 'Taxi,' they look and me and think – they look like, 'Oops! I didn't mean to ask.' They're thinking, 'You're a *taxi driver*!' and I'm thinking, 'Yeah, I know you're thinking that I'm a *taxi driver* but you don't know. You – don't – know. I'm not what you think. You don't know what I know. You

137

think I'm a taxi driver but I'm not daft. I work four hours a day, I've no stress. You might be a businessman or whatever; you might be clocking it but I might be making just as much as you sat on my arse in a car. I've got an easy life. I do what I want.'

Where I work in Leeds, customers are grateful. Some people can't handle it, some people don't know where they are, but they're still grateful: 'Everybody's pissed, there's nobody who's not pissed. Home's ten miles away. There's no way I'm going to get home on my own. Who's going to take me home? There's nobody, only that Asian cabby.'

English people, they could be bastards when they're at work, but when they're going out, they are partying. Nobody's going to stop them, nobody's going to spoil their day. If they want to go to a nightclub and it's twenty pounds to go in, they'll pay twenty pounds to go in. They'll spend one hundred or two hundred a night. They want that whole thing: the curry, the club, the pub, the beer, the taxi. It's all part of their night out.

Some Lulloo

I've had jobs but they never last. That's why they're temp jobs. I've done packing, warehousing and last year I did some time with circuit boards; you know, like assembly line. That were good work. Clean and easy work, but it never lasts. Me, I think I can only get temp jobs because I'm like used to that now. They come through work agency in town but when I'm not working I sign on. Even they tell me to pull all the temp jobs out and call about them. Longest I've been signing on is about two months. At first – first few weeks – it's alright. You hang about, do nowt, piss around, watch telly, listen to some tunes, do more nowt. It kills you after week two, bores you to tears, man. I were ready, I swear, to do myself in! I know some mates and they can hack it. Never mind hack it, they buzz off it, thinking they're winning all because they're getting a few pence off the government for doing nowt. That's foolishness. You gotta do summat, can't just do nowt like some *lulloo*. You gotta be able to keep yourself busy because if you don't, you might as well rub yourself out.

It would be a million times better if I wasn't stuck with temp jobs. But it all comes down to me. If I'd worked when the time were right, I might not be jumping from one temp job to another temp job to another and another and on and on. Might be doing that for all my life, now. I could be doing crap jobs like this 'til I'm eighty! When I were at school, I should have worked more. That's what they all used to say to you when you were at school – 'Sort yourself out, work hard, make something of yourself.' My older brother, he's seven years older than me. We don't always connect, but even he used to give it to me when he looked at my reports: 'Don't fuck around. Now's your chance to learn, to get some education and exams and that. Otherwise you'll end up like me.'

He were working in takeaways in them days. He were even working when he were at school. On weekends, he'd work at my uncle's takeaway in Wakefield and get thirty/forty pound for his time, which were alright for him – young lad, still at school, walking round with forty dollars in his pocket was good going.

He's got a restaurant in Leeds and he's got two houses on rent. He earns enough cash, but he's got family to think about. He got married young. At the time he were right pissed off about it because he were only eighteen or summat. His missus, they brought her over from Pakistan, she were like twenty odd! I laughed. I felt a bit like guilty but I thought it were funny at the time. Dead sad, really. Young lad like him, knowing fuck-all about fuck-all, being forced to marry. Things are alright for them now, though. Happily married and all that. Big semi up by Morrisons, all nicely kitted up – new kitchen, new furniture, all that stuff; nice car. They got two lovely kids – boy and girl.

My brother and his missus, they're fond of each other, got kids and a good life together. But if it were me, I wouldn't take the chance. That's why I'm not married, yet. They've tried, my mum and my dad, to find someone for me, but I know I'm not ready. I says to my mum, 'Look, Mum. Me, I can't look after myself, how am I supposed look after someone else?'

She gives it, 'Give over, everyone says that. Even your brother said that when he got married.'

Then I said to her, 'Yeah, but with him, he had no choice, did he? You *made* him get married. Can't do that to me, 'cos you know what'll happen!'

Meaning I'll do a runner on them! I said it jokingly but she sort of knows I'm being serious as well. I don't believe in that. It's not right. Even my dad's on my side. These days, even he has a go at people whose kids or whatever are getting divorced, giving it, 'It's their own fault'. Because, nine times out of ten, it's because they were forced in the first place. If they hadn't been forced, they wouldn't be getting divorced now. Divorce can happen to anyone who gets married, I suppose, but when you force someone, you're asking for trouble.

My sister, she's still at school. We were talking a while ago about this sort of thing. She knew someone who knew someone – a young lass like her – but in a different school. Her parents were trying to get her married. She were only a kid. For some reason, her mum and dad thought the time were right. Poor lass, I thought. Fifteen, maybe sixteen, and her parents have got it into their head that she needs to get married. People have to get married at some time but not like that. It's wrong – it's your kid, not your fucking slave or someone you hate. I know what they think, that once you get old enough – and mature enough – you should settle down with someone and not fuck about. But you can't force that on people, even your own kids. I know what they say, that you're supposed to obey your parents but your parents, they're supposed to look out for you, too. I don't know what happened with that lass. She should have ran off. It's hard for lads to see it from a girl's point of view but all I have to do is wonder how I'd feel if my mum or dad were planning something like that with my own sister. It wouldn't happen because, my dad, he's learnt his lesson and he's not stupid. He sees what's going on in the world but in case it did happen, if they tried getting my sister married when she didn't want to, then I'd do a mission with her, help her peg it. No question.

I'm still young and I got plenty of time for a family and that. All depends on getting myself settled before I can try settling into a family. Worst thing is work. All comes back to having regular work because without work, you don't have regular money and without money, you're knackered. Everyone needs money. My brother's asked me a few times to come work with him but I don't think so. Don't like the work and we'll only get in each other's ways. We used to argue like mad when we were together and the only reason that's stopped is because we hardly see each other now.

I've still got same bunch of people around me. Grown up together all of us. Went to same schools, same mosque and now we hang around in the same cars and same pads. We got a flat that we all pay for together. Don't do anything silly there – just use it to hang around when we need to: watch videos, listen to music, smoke. We used to just loaf around the street and that but it looks bad and people were complaining to my parents about me and the rest of us. We never did anything – just stood at end of street, chatting and that. Sometimes we got a bit loud and messed around and I think that's what pissed them off, might have scared people off a bit.

It's dull around here, no question about that – boring as anything but probably most places are like that. I like it, though. My patch, my yard. I don't mean I own it or it's mine and no one else can have it. It's something I want to protect and be proud about. Some people support a footy team, I support what's around me. Bradford's my city, Undercliffe is my own backyard. I can't see myself leaving here for anywhere else. A lot of people do move out, though. White people – rich white people and rich Asians – they escape to nice, posher places. Like my uncle and his family, they lived next door to us for years but even they moved out to Thornton last year. My cousin, my uncle's son, he got sorted with a nice computering job so they decided to move. Nicer but smaller house. I suppose that's bound to happen: earn more, want more.

Round here, I do and I don't miss white people. There were some that were really good people and that, so I miss them. I'm Pakistani – well, my parents are proper Pakistani, I'm next generation – but I miss white people's company. When I'm working, that's when I link in with whites. Otherwise I would never talk to them. There's a few who are still here, but there's nothing going on. They'll say 'hi' and 'bye' and you'll say 'hi' and 'bye'. Sometimes I think we should make a bigger effort to show them we're alright. Like my cousin, that's what he says about moving into Thornton – round here it's a bit of a lost cause but places like that, you can make things work. Round here, a lot of people are struggling to keep their heads above water so maybe that's why it's hard to link in.

There were these white people who lived a few doors down. Me and their son, Michael, we were best mates. Went through all school together, even nursery. Good lad, were Mike – a real, nice, decent lad. Had a lot of respect for everyone. Not a racist bone in his body. But they moved out about four/five years ago. Over in Thackley or summat now, they are. I miss them – even his mum and that. Nice people. But some I'm glad have moved out. Right arseholes – pissheads, junkies and that. Some are still here but a lot have been moving out from these few streets for years now. I can't make anyone stay or go, no one can. It'd be nicer if the nice ones stayed and the dickheads fucked off, though!

Prospects aren't brilliant but I'm lucky. I got family and I got my boys: I'll never starve. If things get hard, money-wise, then I can always fall back on my brother and work for him if I really, *really* have to. But I'll see. Part of me's thinking I'm still young and I should have another crack at school, education – get a second wind and do it properly and for myself this time. One of my cousins from Leeds did it like that. He was a bigger dosser than me and older than me when he went to college. Did 'A' Levels then university where he did his degree. He's a pharmacist now and works in a chemist in Leeds. Married, house, kid on the way, *Z3* in the drive – cracked it. So maybe that's a road map I should look at – sort my head out, get some education, get a job, my own house and then settle myself down, have two or three kids. Not a bad plan, but I'll see.

Chill Out

I was born in Leeds Road but I moved to Marshfields when I was about five or six. I don't like to be classed as West Bowling. If you come in our area you'll see two different things. You stay in our area and then you go in West Bowling you're going to be shocked, you're going to think, 'How's this classed as West Bowling? Why is this area classed as West Bowling?' It's just a road, basically. In between there's Manchester Road, and that's it. But West Bowling, I'm not going to lie, it's our own people who are messing it up and making it harder for us.

In our area it's all nicely done out now. No messing about, no houses burning, no cars getting nicked, everybody's safe with everyone. You walk in West Bowling, 'What you looking at?' There are a lot of attitude people there. I don't know if it's because there's a lot of drugs in there or 'cos they think they're big boys. There's some younger ones show you attitude nowadays. That's drugs. When they're hyped up, when they're coked up, when they're drugged up, they think they're the man. It's the drug taking them over and it's not themselves talking like that, it's the drug that's doing the damage. A lot of people use it and that's where the problem is.

I wouldn't say it's just in Bradford, they're everywhere. If you get drugs out, people will be straight as a pencil. If there's no drugs, nobody's going to nick for money to get drugs. All these shooting happenings, what is it over? Drugs. All these enemies, good mates they used to be, good mates in school time, now you hear about them because they've split up because money's got to their mind. Me, I use spliff – that's it, man, nothing else. Once in a while I'll drink booze, only when you're out with the lads for a laugh. Religion's very important, I understand that. We're not strong enough, yet. If we were strong enough we wouldn't be doing none of this shit. If you always follow Islam, all this trouble we're having, we wouldn't be having it. Drinking's a bit out of the way, it's a bit out of hand. It all comes down to your *iman*. If your *iman's* weak then *Shaitan's* going to take control of you. I know what's right and what's wrong and I know what I do. Sometimes, you can't help it. If I go out sober-headed, the problems I've got, they're not going to get out of my head. I want to chill out. You drink to forget but the next day that problem's still going to be there.

It's hard to think about the future, ten/fifteen years from now. What I hope for is for something decent because probably I'll have my own kids. What I'm going through I don't want my kids to go through. I don't want my kids smoking spliffs all the time. It slows your mentality down. It slows you down other ways. When you don't have it, you're going to rattle, it's going to make you do daft shit, it's going to make you do more wrong things.

I got a clean record. If a copper came up right now and asked my details, he'd keep me here half-an-hour/forty-five minutes and he'd get my details out. It happened to me before. There were a few of us lads and we were in town, in a side street. No harm. We were just like chatting and chilling, and we had a few girls round with us as well so it got a bit over-noisy and a bit over-crowded as well. Anyway the girls made all the mess. When they saw the police coming, the girls did a legger. Us lot were just finishing our cigarettes, so we thought let's split it and go. They made us pick up the rubbish. We didn't even do it, but we still had to pick it up otherwise you'd have to go to lock-up for no reason. I was saying to him, 'Take me, I ain't done nothing. What does it say in the law against standing here? If that's not your rubbish, you don't have to pick it up. There's a camera there. I ain't chucked nowt.' I've got all my defence ready. They can't touch me.

My haircut, I used to have it shaven and half shaven, like a Tyson cut – a bit of a line there. I don't sell drugs or 'owt, but I've been called a drug dealer enough times because of my dress style. I look like a drug dealer, especially when I'm proper slickered up. My jewellery that I wear, fat gold, bling bling and all that. But the copper was just checking me on my dress sense. It come down to my details, 'Give me your details. What's your name. Blah-de-blah.'

I give him them and nothing would come up. Nothing. They go, 'No, you're lying to us.'

I go, 'Check *their* details.'

One of my mates gave the same postcode because he lives in the same street and they goes, 'How can that be?'

I give it, 'You muppet, he only lives two doors away. What do you mean *how can that be?*' Daft shit like that, 'Oh, you're blagging us. You're blagging us.'

I go, 'What you going to do? You're wasting my time. Are you going to take me or are you going to let me go?'

They couldn't find my name. After forty-five minutes, they let us go.

I'm working at a takeaway five days a week, just evenings. I used to work in computer accessories – inkjet cartridges and consumables and all that kind of stuff. I got laid off.

I had a stroke – Bell's Palsy. My right side got pulled and my left side was numb. I couldn't move my jaw, couldn't eat. They gave me drugs and treatment – steroids. Eight tablets a day, hardcore for two weeks. Those steroids, they seriously made me lose weight. I'm alright now, but then my family could see it on my face – looked proper sucked in, right gaunt.

I had the Dutch runs – diarrhoea. That's what the hospital says I got it through. They were asking me all these daft questions. They ask you about cold sores and have you ever had one. I says, 'No. What are you on about, man? I never had one in my life, I'm telling you. I'm a normal fit lad, man.' But I'm alright now. You can't even tell. Some people have a bit of it left on their face. I've got a mate, you can tell when he talks, he slurs his speech a bit.

Our lot tell you to look in the mirror a lot, but I didn't do that 'cos that doesn't really work. You need to be in a hot country because the heat hits the mirror and then hits your face. That doesn't really work here. I ate a lot of pigeons and pigeon soup and that stuff. *Alhamdulilla*, I was alright in two weeks. Quick recovery.

I went on sick for two months. I go to the work people, 'Look, I don't know, my doctor gave me a two months sick note but it could take longer. In between, if I feel any better, I'll come in early.'

And they go, 'Alright.'

They did a clever one on me. I come back and I work two days and they sack me. I wanted to leave anyway, man. My brother worked there and I didn't feel comfortable. He's about twenty-four. I don't feel loose when he's there, because he's not that open-minded. Anything I say, he'll go home and tell the family. The other one who's older, he's on a different level. This one, he's just a bit twisted in his head. The one who's older than him, he's on a nice level. I could chat to him, I could chill with him, go anywhere with him.

When I got sacked, I looked for work for about two or three weeks, but you can't find nowt straight away. So then I thought, 'It's summer I'll have a little break.' In my whole life I think I've signed on four times. Told them to shove the book up their arse when I went back to the Job Centre. People like to work in one place and sign on at the same time, so that's what I used to do. I did that for quite a long time. It was alright was that, it was chilled out, as in nowt hard. I used to do nights and you get knackered. I'd have a spliff – it'd give you a nice hardcore sleep. And then I'd have to go to the Job Centre at ten o'clock. That New Deal came out – they'd send you to this other place to help you to do that Job Club shit. I couldn't tell them I was working. If I told them that they could understand why I was waking up late. So the first time I went to that Job Club or whatever they call it, I were about fifteen minutes late. Just fifteen minutes late, man. So the guy sent me back to the Job Centre and said, 'Make sure you're not late next week, otherwise we're going to cut your thingy off.'

So I went the next week and I were about fifteen minutes

153

late again. The man sent me to the Job Centre – and my adviser from the Job Centre sent me back. I went and it was back and forward. I am tired and a bit stressed out, and he sent me back to the Job Centre and he goes, 'What happened?'

I goes, 'You know what? You can have this book and shove it up your arse!'

I chipped out, never been back since.

I'm looking for a good decent job. Summat smart. I don't want to be a taxi driver or a takeaway worker washing pots like other people. If I go to college, now I know myself that in that first month I'll work my arse off. I'm a young lad. The girls, the environment, is eventually going to pull me away. I know I'm going to go and waste time there. What's the point, man?

I never used to hardly go to school. I had a bad reputation. I don't blame the school or anything, I blame myself. Can't blame no one else, I was just a hot-headed little punk. But, *Alhamdulilla*, since I've left school, I've calmed down. If anybody said anything to me, I'd go fight them – that's the kind of person I was then. I'd stand up: 'How old are you? Who are you?' I didn't care. Even if I got battered by ten guys I'd still stand there and try to fight.

In four or five years I should have my own business. I don't know what, but that's what my aim is – to have my own business. You're your own boss, your own mind. You can't just go into it and then in the next two/three months you close down. You want to look at it in the long-term.

Sometimes stress can get to you. Family nagging at you, 'You're doing nothing, you're useless,' this and that. I get that a lot, man. That's why I stay at home majority of the time. But now I start work at five o'clock in the takeaway, that's temporary, and then chill out afterwards with a bunch of lads. Five to twelve, then we chill out. Local lads, have a smoke and that, have a little drive, chill out, chat here and there. After work you want a nice chill, man.

J

Me and my two brothers, the three of us, got married in Pakistan last summer. My eldest brother got married once before and divorced, so he got married again. One of my brothers wanted to settle down. He's twenty-nine, was studying in Manchester doing his Master's degree, but he wasn't really into it. He started it, then about half way through he lost interest and he goes, 'I want to get married, I need an incentive to settle down and sort myself out. By myself, I'm just going to chill out in Manchester. I want to get hitched.' At the time, my family – they asked me. I said, 'Yeah.'

It was really fast. Within two weeks everything was finished. The first week we spent just getting to know them and the rest of the family. Then after day six we did the *nikkahs* – all three in one day. We did two in our village and one about ten minutes away. One in the morning and two in the evening. The good thing was it was organised. I've seen people round here do them and they couldn't organise a piss up in a brewery. Everything's last minute: 'Who's got the registry booked?' or 'Hold on a minute, the groom's not here' or 'The witnesses are not here!' Everybody was already there. We came, we met everybody, we sat down, the *Maulvi* asked us a question three times and all he said was, 'Sign here'. Literally less than five minutes. Before we could change our mind they shackled us up: here's your ball, here's your chain, there you go!

I was there for two months. I'm still waiting for her to come. They have given me a six month waiting time. About two or three months have gone so far. They have this really big form that you have to fill in saying who you are and who she is, how many brothers and sisters she has got, where she lives, where you live, all your brother's and sister's family and everything. I think it's unnecessary information. What they want is proof that you can support her, she's got somewhere to stay. They make it more difficult every time. I can understand why they do it as well: they don't want people coming for no reason whatsoever, just coming to take up space.

As of now, and maybe for the foreseeable future, I will stay with my parents. Two of my brothers are planning on moving out. One is not too sure but he will in the next couple of years. He's about thirty now and my parents want him and his missus to have a place of their own. It would give him a bit of responsibility. Even though he is nearly thirty, he doesn't really have much responsibility on his shoulders. My parents are really happy and satisfied that he's got a job and he's earning money for himself and he's got the ball rolling. Because I'm a bit younger, I'll stay with my parents for the next few years to look after them.

My dad came over in the fifties or sixties. He was working in a textile mill. He used to just tell me when he came over there used to be maybe like ten/twelve of them in one house. They'd work seven days, really long hours, just grinding away. After six weeks they'd take one day off. Now he's got a couple of problems related to work. His hearing is not too good because of the loud machines. When he was about fifty, all the mills closed and everything, and that was his profession. He's been unemployed for the last, at least, fifteen to twenty years because he couldn't get work.

He's not particularly religious or particularly anything. He's up with current affairs that's going on in the state of the world. I wouldn't say I'm religious. I might have an appearance that says I'm quite religious because of my beard. I don't go to clubs or anything like that because it's not part of my scene. I go to the cinema, I go shopping more than most, I go travelling, I do all sorts of stuff. It doesn't conflict with Islam but most people don't really know and they think it does.

A couple of years ago when I had a smaller beard, even then I used to notice it. At that time I was probably like most other youths in West Bowling, didn't know much about anything else outside Bradford, never been anywhere out of Bradford. I think a lot of people in West Bowling are fairly narrow-minded: on a one-track mind, their own thought, how they are, how they think it should be. They all watched that documentary* and as far as they are concerned every white person is a member of the BNP – like the BNP think every Asian is a bloody terrorist or they're savages. Up to a couple of years ago I was really conscious. In Bradford, especially West Bowling, there's not a lot of white people. If you chat to them and speak to them, you find out they are all normal people, they have got nothing against you. The majority of them are not bothered. It's simple: they respect you and you respect them.

If you're a part of West Bowling, even if you just live in West Bowling, then there's an element of some sort of safety. There

* Refers to a documentary entitled 'The Secret Agent' screened in August 2004 on BBC Television.

161

is a lot of crime, drugs and stuff like that goes on. In the last year there's probably a lot more drug dealers sprouted up, and there's a lot more inter-fighting between them. I know guys who used to be friends, used to deal together and one went and started dealing with another one. The two friends are now enemies and fighting against each other. Three or four guys used to hang around on the street corner and they were best friends, and now all four are separate. One's been stabbing the other one's brother. There's a lot more stuff like that going on. I've never seen it happen, but I've seen the results of it. I've seen the victims.

I look around and I think, 'I knew him and I knew him, I used to go to school with him.' It's a lot more common in West Bowling for someone to be a drug dealer than for someone to come home with an 'A' level or a degree. The older lot who started it off, older guys who were drug dealers, they have probably made a lot of money. They sugar-coat it and portray it as glamorous and people think, 'Oh, hold on a minute, he's made so much money.' They don't see the nine drug dealers who got locked up for ten years each. They see the one guy who made some money! That's their role model. It's a sad thing that people like that are role models. Even the ones who are locked up are role models for the ones who aren't. You'll talk to them and they'll say, 'It's alright what we do. What else can we do? We need money.'

A drug dealer, he's not just going to mess himself up. He sells to ten people in a day. It's messing ten people up as well. In West Bowling there's a lot of that. A lot of people make out that the guy who's selling drugs is not doing wrong. It's got to such a stage that they say it's the police who are doing wrong for locking them up. That's the mentality now – a drug dealer is right for selling drugs, but the police are wrong for setting him up. You sit there and they're talking and they say, 'Oh, did you hear what happened to Imran? It was bad news when the police set him up and he got caught with heroin and fifty thousand pounds. Look how bad it was, man. He's got locked up for *nine* years. I hate the police, Imran never did anything. Imran's a good guy.' And I sit there and I think, 'Listen to what you're saying.' Imran isn't that good a guy because he's selling seven kilos of heroin in West Bowling and he's got fifty thousand pounds cash. Where's that seven kilos going to go? Someone's going to take it. It's not just going to disappear.

West Bowling, apart from the drug dealers, it's really nice. Them aside, it's a tight-knit community. Everybody knows everybody, it's like a village atmosphere. I have a problem with police harassing people. In West Bowling, they will pick on someone they have no hold on, or they will pull him for something small. They know who's doing what and who's not. For some reason they knocked on my door and they came and they said, 'Something's happened and this address has been given, and we're looking for someone called J.'

I said, 'No one called J lives here.'

I don't know what they were looking for, it was like they were just fishing for something. They had no description of the guy they were looking for. They just had a name – it's not even a name, it's like an alias – J. This police officer was adamant for me to go and sit in the back of his van. I did not want to do that. A week before, they'd grabbed my brother off the streets so I thought they might be following up on him. They roughed him up a little bit, stuck him in the back of a van, just slammed the door and locked him up for four hours and sent him home at six in the morning on *foot patrol* from the station. Now they come to my house and the officer goes, 'Come and sit in the van.'

And I goes, 'I can answer your questions just as well here as I can in your van.'

My older brother came down and then he goes, 'Look, don't give him any grief. Just go and stand outside their van and we'll see what they've got to say.'

So I went in and sat in the van and my brother stood outside. All they did was take my name and details and run it through their computer.

I've walked around other areas in England and I have never seen as many police as I've seen in West Bowling. I see vans and *foot patrol* and cars and all sorts driving around at all times. I don't know why they do it. I don't know what their reason is. It doesn't make me feel any safer. All it makes me think is there's something happening. If it's not the police, it's the people they are looking for.

Nothing To Declare

I was supposed to go to attend my sister's wedding. She's younger than me. It was all sorted out and arranged. She actually convinced my mum and my dad that she wanted it. Nobody forced her to do it. Even up until the last day before I went to Pakistan, I kept asking her, 'Are you happy?' I knew that there was infiltration – she'd gone there on her own and they somehow influenced her head.

I went first, my mum and my sisters were supposed to follow, and my dad shortly after them. About a week before they were due to come, I went and booked the hotel. So everything's done. I get a phone call and it's my sister and she's fucking beefing on the phone about she doesn't want this marriage, and she doesn't want this and she doesn't want that. First of all, I were shocked. My mate here, I rang her, and I said to her, 'Keep an eye on her.' A few days later just before they were about to come, she's ringing me. It's like she's wanting me to do something. I said, 'What am I supposed to do?' I still felt bad. The next thing I know, she goes, 'I'll nick my passport.'

My dad rings up. The passport's gone. Nobody could find it. My mum and dad actually believed that it had got lost; she had them convinced. I knew otherwise even though she didn't admit it to me. Some knob-head had been messing with her head and promising her stupid things, like mansions and cars and this, that and the other. Really screwed with her head. I didn't want it, particularly that she gets married there, in Pakistan, and neither did my dad. All she had to do was just say.

My dad wouldn't want to put any of us through that. He somehow conjured up that she had exams or something and it wasn't possible for her to come now, that she can't come and it can't happen. It took a week to get it out and everything, to sort it out. But eventually they did and it didn't happen. I had to put up with everything that was going on there, with my mum and everybody. Then I sent them back and I was there on my own. That place is not nice.

I went to Pakistan when I was really young, once when I was in Middle School, and I went once when I finished school. When I went to Pakistan this time, despite all the rest of the shit, I knew there's places worth seeing. K2 – nineteen hours we drove in a jeep, got to this settlement. From there to get to K2 you've got to walk four days.

It was so beautiful. I know I love that place but I got robbed there, I got poisoned there. On the way back, I got so pissed off I wanted to smack them bastard Customs lot. He's looking in my bag like I've done summat wrong, like I'm a criminal or summat. Three groups of *gorays*, trekkers and geography teachers are walking through: they didn't open their bags, they didn't check their bags, they went straight onto the plane. For all we knew they could have been terrorists.

I don't know what I am. I'm just lost, that's what I am. I haven't got a recognised identity. I don't associate with what's been set. I don't associate with totally British: I'm not *gora* and yet if someone says I'm Pakistani, I'm not. British Asian, but I don't think that term justifies it. It doesn't mean much, man. People can't understand that because for me going back there, this time was a shocker – the people and everything.

I'm going through Customs and I'm trekking these DVDs. I say they are for myself and for my mates, gifts and stuff like that. They won't let me go. I go, 'You deal with this however you want to deal with it, yeah.'

He goes, '*Tthhree pownd.*'

I said, 'We earn it as well. If you wanted, you could just let me go right now. It won't mean fuck-all to you. You're just using this to bully me.'

I ended up giving him money. He goes, 'I'm not going to have any problem ahead.'

Next man stops me. I give him some money.

A third guy stopped me. I just blew up. I'd just had it to there with everything going on at home – proper fired up. I just flipped on him. I started saying, 'You let *goray* go. In that country, I get the same shit – they get treated better than I do. Why do you think that people don't like this country? It's because of fuckers like you.'

There was a journalist there and the guy gets his camera out and starts taking pictures. I was shouting, 'I want to see the manager! I give that fucker over there money! I give *him* money and now *you're* asking me for money, too! You're not letting my stuff go through! What kind of shit is this?! I've got no money left on me because you've taken it all!'

For the first time I actually felt, 'I love that place.' Not just Bradford but UK – Britain – as a whole. My mates, when they've gone abroad, they always say they're from Leeds, not from Bradford. It sort of pisses me off. What's Leeds? You live in Bradford.

I got back: *Customs – Nothing to Declare*. The guy here, the Customs guy, he comes up to me, and the way he addressed me, I just felt like kissing him. The guy, he goes, 'Excuse me, mate? Are you alright? Have you had a nice holiday? Are you travelling on your own?' I actually felt good. The guy's asked me nicely. I had more than enough cigs, I'd lots of DVDs and that, I even had some display Samurai swords. I didn't think they'd get through. He put them through, and I think in the end he was so relieved that I didn't have drugs on me – the guy's clean – that he actually let everything go. He just said, 'I'll let them go, it's your property but the police might have a problem with it.' I just wanted to hug the guy.

Those things what pissed me off back over there exist here. This whole culture thing – this caste system – what they believe in so much, that really does my nut in. When you're from a certain caste, as far as my understanding goes, it's an application of the way that your ancestors lived in Pakistan. When you come here, that doesn't apply. Most of us live on that working-class level. Everybody's the same, but yet there's still that sort of thing. My mate got married the other day. The guy brought a horse and a *dolee* to carry the bride from one street to another – make sure you tell the whole world. Being above someone, putting somebody down, just trying to be better and showing everybody else, that's the most important thing – that people see it.

People are constantly trying to bring another man down. He's doing well or he's doing something good, or he's doing

170

something different. There's like a movement of MCs in Bradford. These guys, they wanted us to do a showdown up at the Theatre In The Mill. They hired it out and it was supposed to be like a battle between us lot and them lot.

It's like me and my mate, we were seen as a bit dodgy: 'What are them two doing?' We went down there. And the amount of hate that I saw frightened me. We felt threatened. It just sounded like there was going to be a kick-off. I hadn't done nothing wrong to none of them people. Most of them used to be my mates. They were so ignorant and so thick. They started rhyming: 'You mother fucker, you this, you that.' All the typical stuff that we try to move away from when we do our rhymes. They were well pissed off because they were outclassed in every single way. They were just ignorant, all they knew to do was swear.

We're writing stuff all the time. We share the workload. Most of the songs as regards the verses, the lyrics and everything, I more or less look after that. But now I'd say it's more like fifty-fifty with everything. He writes his own stuff, and we come up with our own ideas for music and we look at the lyrics and put them together. Then we go into the studio. We have one sheet of paper which tells you the structure of songs, how's its going to go. We start putting it together with the beat first and then we look for some sounds, just get the main part of the beat, how we want the beat, what kind of beat we want. Most of the beats don't end, we just keep adding and taking off.

I do a lot of travelling but I'm on hold at the moment. I haven't left many places out: America, Switzerland, Poland, Lithuania, all over Europe, France, Greece. When the youth club stopped I just carried on because I knew the links and the way to do things. I organised things myself after that.

I value Bradford more when I travel out. When I went out to Pakistan I valued Britain as a whole, just wanted to come back here. When I travel around England if I stay in different places, then I value Bradford because I know that it's home. I know that my corner shop's going to stay open until one o'clock in the morning. It's just a security thing, about belonging as well – this is my place and this is where I live. You lose that when you go away.

I'd done a youth exchange to Poland and got in touch with this Lithuanian group. One of them had a band and me and my mate managed to raise some money, and we went across for a two week visit, chilling with them. I went and met this group, a rock band, and they wanted me to play some songs with them. They goes, 'There's some concerts coming up in two cities in Lithuania.' I said, 'Yeah, cool.' I didn't have a clue what sort of scale these lot were. I just thought they were some corner street band.

I went in the morning and there was nobody there at that time. This huge park. Right at the end they were building the stage and they put the frame up, and I go, 'That looks a bit big.'

And they go, 'Yeah, there's a concert here. Do you think we're going to put tables up or something?'

The guys were *known*. Instead of putting my backing music on and just going on, they could pick out sounds and stuff. A hip hop track, they could play it on a bass guitar and drum kit. We just did it like that. They would be doing their shit and I'd be doing my shit. By the end, I had security guards escorting me to the stage. I was the only *aapna* and they got to know me. The birds were hot on it, couldn't get their hands off me. I felt like I were superstar here – all the security guards, all these birds there, this, that and the other. It were surreal, but I'm so glad I had that experience, man. Thanks to them bastards. They invited me back again as well and I did another one. I went on stage, I got backup dancers and all this shit.

I want to do well. One of the reasons is not just for me but for the people around me, my family. I wanted to keep the music on the boil for a bit but I need some sort of security. I'm not saying that I need a record deal that's going to guarantee me so much money. The problem now is that I haven't got the security from nobody.

People I hang around with, I don't identify with the dress, the language, everyday habits and things what they do. I don't identify with that stereotype. Their lives are just based around smoking weed and that's it, nothing else. You've got to have this talk and a presence about yourself. It's meant to be very threatening. They just need to put up this front. Insecure about themselves because they think that the world is against them in a big way. If there are opportunities there, instead of taking them up, chill out.

We used to live with my grandma in Girlington. It's safe for me because all the drug dealers and all the gangsters are my school mates from when we were younger. They're everywhere, man. It bothers me because I live there. My little cousins, and maybe one day my kids, are going to live there. I'm not confident that is going to die out, it seems like it's getting stronger and stronger at the moment. It's the money thing, definitely. It's a culture thing as well, being cool. Fifteen/sixteen year olds, they're all in that culture where they're just smoking weed, that's all they're doing. Even myself, when it comes to a gig or something like that, I might do a bit, half a joint or something like that. I'm not reliant on it, not addicted to it. It's not something I enjoy doing all the time. The thing is, it's something what's become a part of their life. When they wake up they're thinking, 'Okay, tonight we need to make a raise.' A *raise* as in raise some cash. Then the next thing you do you go and buy your beer, and then you sit round and get smoked out until you're dropping, and then you go home.

People are on heroin. It's just that the people on heroin is what you don't see. It's what they're making their money from – a lot of money. Dope is what everybody's selling to the kids, an everyday drug what everybody buys all the time. There's a lot of people deal weed. Those are not going to make a million. The big fish are people you don't see, the real drug dealers. There's a few of those. It is a career in a big way. You have a look at the guy and he is a role model now to the young kids living in our area. And the guy never went to school. He dropped out before sixteen, got kicked out. I used to be at his house trying to get him to school but he wouldn't go. He never worked in his life, and yet he's managed to open up the biggest business selling the best cars and is able to do anything. There's a whole image that goes with it, 'I'm not a girl, I'm not a pussy, I'm a bad boy me, I'm going to do this, I'm going to do that. I'm going to drive around. I'm going to always have attitude. I'll have a chip on my shoulder. I'm going to hit the cops. I'm going to do everything illegit but I'm going to make it.' Maybe it's like an unconscious rebellion against the system. But it's the community that's suffering – the young people. Mothers, fathers, they've lost their sons and they're suffering the most. There's a lot of tragic stories in there as well – people who've died from overdoses, people who have been beaten up, people who have been killed.

Friction

I see it getting worse with the youngsters, their attitude, the way they are, a chip on their shoulder. They seem hard-done-by or something. I was brought up in a strict environment. Nowadays you can see kids hanging around the street until midnight even at a young age. When I was growing up, I had to be in at a certain time, and if I had to go somewhere I had to tell my father. What I see is parents who are working, I'm not saying 24-7, but they are working and they don't seem to be bothering about their kids. All they are concerned about is bringing the bread in.

When I was growing up, I used to hear about Leeds Road and West Bowling/East Bowling being a bit rough. But now, I don't know whether it's because of drugs, it just seems totally different. When I was growing up, say you were going out with a girl or summat, you wouldn't dare be seen in case some of your relations see you. They don't give a toss. They will be walking round hand in hand. I see it as being respectful. If someone older did actually say summat to me, I probably wouldn't even say anything back to them. But now, if you said summat to them they'd probably tell you to eff off.

There's some parts of London you can't go. Kensington, you think it's a posh, expensive area, but there's a bumming dole office there. Drunks – every morning there's a scrap, more or less. East London – really rough. Even Hounslow, there's drugs there. You think in Bradford that drugs go on. In London, what I've seen there is drugs, pimping, everything. Where I live, Hounslow, there's a lot of Sikhs doing it. I've seen a lot of alcoholics with the bottles coming out of subways in the morning when I'm just going to work. Some of the rough areas, there's always trouble. But now that the property prices have boomed, a lot of them are working and have two or three jobs. They haven't got time to mess about like they did before. It's sort of taken a certain percentage of it out – they are now all working. There's obviously none of that where they've got time to do stupid things or drugs or whatever. I was reading this article in the Sunday papers – house ownership. Sikhs were on top and we were at the bottom. I always thought 'bricks and mortar', your parents drill into you. Asians are moving into more affluent areas as well. Asians move in, the *gorays* move out. I've heard they're moving towards Bingley and that. It's good in a way, more interaction with other communities.

I knew this Sikh girl. I was quite surprised, but her parents were forcing her to get married, giving her a lot of stress, grief and everything. Muslims, they just sort of agree to it really – 'Oh, sod it' – just to keep their parents happy rather than upset them. My father, he's passed away. He probably would have kicked my arse and got me married by now! He took me a few places and that, but I kept saying 'no'. I went to relations, to a wedding. I remember once when I went to Newcastle and I didn't really look because I wasn't interested.

A lot of the older generation have worked hard, seven days

a week. It was just work and that were it, work and save. The younger generation are probably spending the money on houses. Before it used to be just any ordinary car, but now, more than whites, the most prestigious cars would be Asians. I wonder if that's causing friction. I think *gorays* look at Asians and think, 'How did they get that car?' When I see Asians I presume there are some who do work hard and deserve what they've got. Some have worked hard for it and some have done it the other way. It's nice to see Asians with nice cars. It shows the *gorays* that Asians have reached a certain point where they are actually working hard and getting on.

When I go down south, what I mostly miss is my nephews and nieces. I always look forward to seeing them when I come back up. I miss Bradford when I haven't been up for a while. I've got a mate who works for an airline and he gets concession tickets, so we just tend to go all over. I've been everywhere. I'd always want to come back.

I always try to give a positive attitude about Bradford when someone asks me down south. I've been born here, it feels like home. I've come to see some of my mates, have a bit of a laugh. It's nice, that feeling. You don't get that down south. Obviously you know people, but you don't get the sort of homely feeling like you do in Bradford.

London Asians, they think of Bradford as backward in the way we live, that we're not progressing as much. They think it's just a dive really. This is a *gora* – a white man's – picture of Bradford. You know the advert when he goes into work, they're humming that music, cobbled streets, just taking the mickey: Arkwright. That's there. We're still living in the dark ages in Bradford. We've got black and white TVs. I've been down south for probably about four years now. When I come back I think Bradford is progressing. Whenever it comes on the news or 'owt, it's always something negative, like riots and that — everybody knew about that down south.

Undercover

I was surprised. You don't really hear about it happening local, in England. It's surprising because you only hear about it happening in different countries. When it happens on your doorstep, it's scary, especially when they got them from Beeston – that's worse, they're coming closer. But why London? Why not anywhere else? Why not Bradford? Why not Leeds?

I got family in London – they work there, so it was a bit scary. The time that it happened, it was early in the morning with a lot of people about. They were down here, about a week before it happened, and they were talking about traffic in London – saying you can't really get about because they got congestion charges in the town centre.

What I don't understand is, they killed innocent people. And if they were really Muslims – I don't know – it just doesn't go together. Killing their own people. Obviously, if a person is going to go and kill himself – a bomb on a bus or whatever – he's gonna know that there's Muslims on this bus as well. Even if there weren't, it still would have made it unfair.

Jihad, that's what they call it, that's why they do it. They think they're doing Jihad and they're gonna go to heaven. I was watching something where they had prisoners in Iraq or Iran or somewhere. They were proper terrorists but they caught them before the bombs went off. When they got them, even they were saying that to do proper Jihad – to be a martyr – if you haven't got that in your heart, if you're doing it because you think, 'I'm gonna go do it, gonna go kill myself because I'm gonna go to heaven,' if that's the reason you're doing it, it's wrong. You've got to do it from your heart to say, 'Yeah, I'm doing it for my country – they're killing innocent people.' But the way this lot are doing it, I don't think it's right because they're killing innocent people, Muslims in the process.

The people who got these young lads to do it, they're from *Madrassay* in Britain. Teachers have been talking to these young lads – telling them about it. These people who become terrorists, they go to their own classes and stuff in their own time – people's houses, try to keep it undercover. So you're scared because you think your mosques and *Madrassay*, what if they start closing them down? Our parents go to mosques to read but they haven't done nowt wrong. Me, I think they're just brainwashing these young lads. Most of them are what? Nineteen to twenty – twenty-one, twenty-two? Just young lads, some of them have just left school. Jihad, it might be okay, but for the right reasons.

News

Closest thing to Pakistan abroad is probably Bradford. Manningham's very Pakistani. I don't think that's a problem. It's been publicised so much as being a mini-Pakistan, an Asian place. People who've got a perception of Manningham from the media's point of view, I don't see none of that. You'll get an odd bit of bother here and there, which you do anywhere. How bad can it be? Why is this a high risk crime area? I cannot understand. I don't know why.

It is to do with the comfort zone really. I'd probably feel a bit weird if I were from up Leeds Road, thinking this is a shit hole. Gangs, kids really, hanging about together. From what I know, from the people I work with, everybody else is doing it, so it's accepted. Two are doing it, third and fourth will be just sitting in the car with them cruising. When he sees them making the money, he says, 'I'm here, I'll do it as well.' That's the kind of thing that's happened up there.

The place, the reputation that has been ruined all over the world, is Manningham. Manningham isn't half as bad as what people make it out to be. Look at Buttershaw, look at flipping Wibsey, at Ravenscliffe. I wouldn't let my cat walk through Ravenscliffe because I know he wouldn't come back out. Look at Eccleshill – supposed to be a good area – look at the state of that. Thackley, Windhill, Shipley, all supposed to be good areas. What's good about them? I know what they're really like, but they don't get media priority.

I've stopped watching news. It used to drive me insane. I stopped watching it and it doesn't bother me any more. I'm not on about just Bradford, I'm on about a world scale. Middle East, Iran, Iraq. It bothers me because of the double standards. It used to stress me out so my solution to that was to cut it out. To a lot of people it might sound ridiculous, burying your head in sand, but it worked for me and it was blissful for a while. Because you belong to Islam, it does hurt. Whether it's here, whether it's in Iraq, Afghanistan, Mars, wherever it is, your way of life is being tarnished. The way you are, the way your family is, everything in your life, the way it is, what you believe in, it's being dragged through the mud. Feeling powerless and not being able to do anything about it makes you a lot more angry. Islam doesn't teach you any violence or anything like that. All it teaches you is to stand up for your rights and for yourself.

After the riots I thought it can't get any worse. But they had the same problem in Leeds, Harehills. No difference, really. It got out of hand. I thought it was harsh, but something had to be done about it. It was getting out of line, out of order. The guy across the road, he got three years. I was talking to him the other day. Made a big mistake – threw a few bricks, learned his lesson, made him a better person. He admits it himself as well – just got carried away with it all. If they'd let them off with that I think Bradford would have been a lot worse.

With 7/7, initially I was just getting information in dribs and drabs. A colleague, one of her friends actually died in it. She didn't know that then. Obviously with her family being around where all this happened – Kings Cross – they all use that. She was really agitated, really worried, getting calls and ringing her family and everything to see if everything was okay. It was a shock, that it happened. We were half expecting it because the media had prepared us for it, really, saying it's inevitable, it's gonna happen. The most shocking thing: British born Muslims did it. That was a shocking bit, really. Don't think it really hit us 'til we got back home and watched the news and realised the seriousness of it, how much devastation it had caused. It was sad.

The media, they divided it, they did make it them and us – blatantly. I felt it. What they were trying to do was, 'These Muslims are your responsibility. You lot should have taken care of them. These extremists are your responsibility, you should have reported them to the police, you should not have allowed this to happen.' What do you mean, *they're your responsibility*? How are they *our* responsibility? Worst thing I felt was why we had to justify what happened. I've got nothing to justify to anybody. It was just four people who went and did something terrible. It's wrong; it shouldn't have happened. It was shocking. Then all the conspiracy theories started coming out. That it was all a set up, these four lads have gone down to London, booked return tickets – suicide bombers booking return tickets, what the hell's that about? And apparently he put a pay and display ticket on their car in the car park: come back and pick it up? God knows, it could be a million things. Whatever happened, it made me feel, 'Why do I have to justify what these people have done? I've got nothing to justify to nobody.' And it upset me. Even watching these so-called Muslim leaders going on air and trying to justify Islam and being a Muslim. They were dancing to the tune. To most of the people that I've talked to, it feels as if they're just there to get their own careers – what you see on the screen, the so-called Muslim Council, the leaders and the politicians and what have you, trying to make an excuse through Islam – that Islam does not condone stuff like this, doesn't tolerate it, which is obvious, blatantly obvious. The worst thing is having to justify what these four people did or having me, as a Muslim, to justify it. 'You're a Muslim, how can another Muslim do that?' How the hell am I supposed to know! Go ask them! That you're all one, intertwined, and you know exactly what happens in your community. Apologising. Why should I have to apologise? A Christian, a Jew – they don't have to apologise for anything that goes on around the world. That's what annoyed me the most about it – it was terrible what happened. It's sick, really – innocent people dying. It wasn't a race thing, it wasn't a religious thing. You look at the papers – there's Muslims in there that have been killed – it was indiscriminate. So why have they made it a race or religious issue? If somebody goes and says I've done it in the name of Islam, then that doesn't make it so.

It has affected me. I think it's affected everybody I know. You do feel it with people you meet. Somebody asked me – one of the passengers in the cab, 'What do you think of the bombings?' I went ballistic on him. I said, 'What do you mean *what do I think of the bombings*? What do *you* think of the bombings?' He says, 'You know, they were wrong – this, that and the other – but you know, what do you think?' I said, 'What do you *want* me to think? What do you want me to *say* to you? You idiot, I think exactly the same way as what you do.'

Leeds, the atmosphere just went bad everywhere. Cabbying, a lot of them were frightened to go to work for the backlash – they didn't go to work for a couple of weeks, thinking what's gonna happen to them. Loads of drivers I've talked to have said that they've had a lot of abuse from passengers or even from people walking past saying, 'You fucking terrorists! You're all the same.' Personally, apart from that one guy, I've been spared – nobody's said anything and nobody's even mentioned it in any way whatsoever. I've been fortunate in that way but I know a lot of them haven't because when you talk to them afterwards they'll say this is what's going on.

In everything else, anything that goes on, the first thing that you've got to is look for the cause. What's causing all this? In this, they're saying, 'No, we're not bothered about the causes, it just shouldn't have happened.' It's making it a bigger divide in the community, within Britain. It's harder to be a Muslim now, even to be Brazilian, let's face it. Poor guy, probably never set foot in a mosque. Just because he was brown skinned. And look at all the lies that the police tried to cover their tracks with. It was an assassination, there's nothing else to it. I don't know whether it was a trigger happy cop or whether it was an order from the top or whatever it was but there was no need for what happened. It shouldn't have happened. The guy wasn't armed, he wasn't dangerous, he didn't jump no barriers, he didn't run – he was sat on his seat in the train. He was actually restrained by one of the officers and while he was restrained they shot him. I tell you what, I wouldn't run with a back pack on and, in winter, I'm gonna wear a t-shirt – see through clothes. Imagine what that poor man's family's going through. Just an innocent victim. I don't know whether it was to send a message out to the rest of the brown skinned people – there's no mercy.

This will take a long time to mend. There'll be people thinking this is the end. A lot of our elders are worried we're gonna get thrown out. People have been saying it for years, the older generation, but we never believed it. But I don't know, there's a little bit inside you that thinks: maybe. Starting on foreign nationals now, who knows where it'll end? Everything has a little starting point and the laws start expanding from there.

Your family is your strength. Look at a building and the strength is in the foundations. If the foundations are weak it's going to crumble. And your foundations – your strength – is in your family, in your discipline, how you are at home, how your parents bring you up, and how they stay with you through life. But parents turn a blind eye: 'He don't listen, I'm sick of telling him, I can't be bothered with him.' That's the kind of thing you get. My kids, I teach them to be respectful. Not just my kids, but my nephews and that as well. The lot of them – half the street is mine. They'll come and shake hands and say *Asalamoalaikum*. They know to respect their elders, they will not swear because I don't swear. A lot of parents, and I've actually heard this, 'Oh, you fucking bastard!' And they expect the kids not to behave in that way. Parents are your foundation. If your foundations are weak you can't build nothing.

It's a taboo subject. 'No, it's not their fault.' How can it not be their fault? How can a sixteen year old kid come home with brand new trainers at one/two hundred pounds, dressed up with kit? Go out, driving whatever, not come home 'til twelve or one o'clock at night? Fathers don't give them nothing, mothers don't give them nothing. Stop for a minute. You haven't got a job, you don't do nothing, you go to bloody *school*. Where are you getting the money for all this? Whose fault is it? They are not stupid. Most of them know. Most of them can't be bothered with the inconvenience that their son might rebel: more bother. A lot just cannot be arsed: 'I'm not bothered about ya, do what ya want, with age it will come, I was like that when I was a kid.' A parent can easily turn round and say, 'Why is it my fault? I don't tell my kids to go out and rob and stuff like that.' It's lack of action. They are a minority but they will become a majority if it's left to them. It does have an effect. Overall I think there is a lot more good than bad. In this area I would say that ninety-five percent of the lads are good. But over time, five percent will probably get to six, seven, eight, nine, ten percent.

I don't think I could move out of Bradford and live anywhere else. It's that comfort zone thing again. Why would I want to move out of Bradford. What for? I don't have no inconveniences here. Why would you want to go and start off somewhere at my age? You're settled, you're happy, kids are doing well at school. People think, 'Oh, this school's a failing school. They're all Asians here, it's not doing 'owt.' My friends as well, they say, 'I'm going to send my kids to a better school because there are not that many Asians there.' That's a status symbol with a lot of Asian people. I remember when we were at school: black people, white people, everything. But you look at it nowadays, they don't know how to deal with each other: he's English, he's Pakistani, he's Indian. We never even thought of them issues when we were at school.

Impact

I woke up and turned the TV on. At that point they only mentioned Edgeware Road and the bus. I can't remember them mentioning any of the others at the time. They didn't actually talk of it as being an explosion. They were unsure so they weren't really mentioning it. I was worried for my cousin because he travels into London. For that week after, I kept bumping into my mates and talking to them, but it didn't have that impact, like 9/11 did. It didn't stir up that same emotion because of the speeches afterwards – and yet, this was only two hundred miles away whereas that was in another country, across an ocean. When 9/11 happened, for the next few months I was thinking, 'Shit! This is really bad. I won't be able to travel, people will look at me.' This time around, I don't feel as much like that, even though it's happened here. Maybe it's because the media's got a bit more objectivity. Because we were getting American feeds with the other one, and you actually see it – the planes going into a tower – with this, you just hear about it. Like they say, a picture paints a thousand words.

For people to do that, they need a lot of organisation. There were four different bombs. To be that intelligent and be that organised, why would you think it was right at the same time? I was a bit dumbfounded by that. You're very clever in doing that, but if you have that much intelligence, wouldn't you have enough intelligence to know what you were doing is wrong?

I get a bit annoyed at some of our spokespeople. They're over gracious and it annoys me: 'I'm very sorry, I'm very sorry, I'm very sorry, I'm very sorry.' It's the same with Musharraff in Pakistan. He came out with, 'You can't kill anyone innocent because if you kill one innocent, it's like killing the whole of mankind.' But the thing is, when he did say that, he failed to mention that he was killing people without questioning them, killing them saying they were suspected terrorists! It's fair enough to condemn it but it goes too far, gets on my nerves, these people being overly gracious – kind of taking responsibility. They're saying we are all Muslims so we're kind of responsible for it and we're sorry for it. You should condemn it but at the same time you should mention where the motives come from. The motives come from injustices.

Muslims have to live in the rest of the world. When it happened, I was totally against it – maybe because we live here, but also because when you live here, you're not being oppressed, there's no danger of any harm coming to you but as a result of this it's more of a chance now, because it's happened.

Full Circle

9/11. I got a text message off my mate, 'There's been an aeroplane flown into Twin Towers.' I texted back saying, 'No, that is a joke.' He says, 'No, it's true.' Ring home, Mum and Dad goes, 'It's terrorists.' Oh no! Second one. Totally shocked. 7/7, sat at work and someone goes, 'There's been bombs in Underground.'

'You what?'

'Bombs in Underground.'

Straight on the phone home – 'Put Ceefax on now!'

Yeah, it's happened but they don't tell everything straight away. I was giving a running commentary to everybody in the office. I was just sat there thinking to myself, '*Nangee gayanh, fir utheh ney utheh poacheeh gayanh* - here we go again!' That's what's happened, we've gone full circle. You get over one atrocity – one bad thing happening, start rebuilding relations and then it happens again. Diabolical. If you think about it, and I'm not talking about physical harm, but who got hurt? Pakistanis did – as a community, Muslims. I'm not very religiously inclined but I do believe in right and wrong and that were wrong. These lads from Keighley were on *Look North* and they were sat there and one of them were saying, 'Yeah, what's happened is really, really bad.' And then he just started barking on about Afghanistan. I wouldn't have done it because I wouldn't have known what to say. I sat there thinking he's got a great opportunity but what he was trying to say was that all this happened over here, but what about what happened in Afghanistan? *They're not asking you about Afghanistan. They're asking you about what happened over here!* Fucking hell, he was doing my head in. People will look at this – BNP will be rubbing their hands with this.

The BNP are getting clever – reeling people in. These guys, they're not good people – they don't promote an equal life. On the BNP website, they've now angled it away from black people to Muslims. Why? Once Muslims are out, the Sikhs are next – then the next. That's how they want to do it – peter them out like that. I used to play football for a team up Haworth and the BNP were recruiting up there. And the players go, 'If I didn't know you, I would do it. If I didn't know you, I would go up and see what it's about. It's because I know you, it'd be an insult to our friendship and all that.' I go, 'You don't know what that means. Thank you very much.'

When I were a kid, Keighley were NF headquarters. When I went to Middle School you couldn't go play in the main playground because white people were there. Every time you went to the fair you got chased out of it; there was fighting. All the time. The thing that is different now is that a lot of both communities – white and Asian – have grown up together and a lot of the white young ones understand it. Obviously there are gonna be some people that will never change – them you've just got to ignore. You just got to let them get on with their existence and you get on with yours; you can't interact. No matter how hard you try they will not accept it. So leave it. Keep going back, that will make them hate you even more. Just leave them be and let them live with their lives – if that's what they want, that's what they want. The others, the ones that have grown up with Asians, these lads, these people aren't like that. There will be some now who think, 'Bloody hell, maybe they are all like that.' I'm not fearful of an uprising or anything like that – anti-Muslim uprising. The only thing that I am fearful of is a tiny little thing: there might be people out there with doubt.

A lass at work said it after the 7/7 bombings. A conversation started, they were on about bombs and all this and one of the Pakistani lads, straight away jumped in with both feet, 'You can't be saying all this stuff. How can you say all Muslims are bad?'

'We're not saying all Muslims are bad. We're just saying a lot of people have been tarred with the same brush, now.'

And I'm like, 'What are you doing, man? *Talk* to these people – don't rant and rave at them. These are the people that you should be talking to about it, they're your workmates – let them know how you feel. Calm down, lad.' I goes, 'I'll tell you straight, maybe people will think twice when they see an Asian guy wearing a backpack. Sounds pathetic, but maybe people will. Hell, even I might look at it twice. If I'm walking around with a backpack, I'm gonna get noticed. It's life, now. Be prepared and deal with it. Jumping in with both feet isn't going to change someone's perception.'

Bombs aren't racist – they don't pick religions. Manchester, I drove through Manchester after the bombs – the ones that went off in the city centre; IRA, years ago. Made me sick. Bombs don't discriminate. So don't think these bombers are heroes. They're no heroes to nobody, they're no martyrs. They are what is ridiculous. People that have had losses – and I mean the actual people in Afghanistan, Iraq – whoever has had atrocities done against them – Palestine, Israel – I don't give a damn which country, which faith; all these people have lost somebody, they've suffered a loss, they're in pain. If I was in their shoes, I'd be bawling my eyes out. When you've felt pain like that, things happen in your head. Can't comment on that – never felt that, but you think to yourself that going out and taking someone else's family, what is that gonna accomplish? Not gonna make you feel better, is it? Not gonna bring your family back, is it? Doing that to somebody else's family accomplishes absolutely nothing because all you've got is somebody who's crying the way you cried and all you've done is killed somebody who's done nothing to you. The guy who dropped the bomb or shot or maimed or killed or whatever, you've done nothing to his family. You've just got another innocent, like you. Doesn't gain anything. Every time I watch the news, I just sit there thinking I'm in this tiny little island, away from all that – used to be away from all that. I don't know how you can solve these problems but they're just getting bigger and bigger and bigger and that's what's scary.

Spin

My dad came here in sixty-five/sixty-six, something like that. He came with nothing much, like they all did. There was my dad, then his brother came a few months later, then his brother-in-law – my mum's older brother. When I used to live with my parents, they used to all come over and they'd talk about what it was like in them days. I wonder how they survived it all. I used to sit there listening to them. Imagine it, you come to this country – you've never even seen it before, and all you've got in your head is what people are telling you and what you're seeing in newspapers and books back home. I bet most of them wouldn't have even been able to find the country on a map, never mind know about the culture, the language or anything. That's a big deal. That took a lot of balls. It's like me getting a rocket and flying off into space, towards some unknown planet. You're risking a lot. How do you know what it's like there? You don't. You're just hopeful that it'll be alright.

I've talked with people of my dad's generation about it and it wasn't as if they were desperate to come here. It was a chance, an opportunity. They were surviving in Pakistan. They didn't come here because they were starving or had nowhere to live. If you ask them, most of them had enough, most could have lived in Pakistan for the rest of their lives. They came here to earn more, that's all. My dad, he told me that's how he thought it would happen: earn, save and go back as a made man. A wealthy, successful man.

My dad, he used to always be going on at us – me, and my brothers especially because they were older. Read. Not just read, but learn, educate yourself. 'It'll work for you, these things. This education in this country is the best in the world and you should do whatever you can to get it. Put it to some use. There's nothing bigger than *thaleem*.' He was right. Knowledge and education, you can't beat it. Learning, that's the word; open your mind and keep taking it all in. If you get it, then everything's there for you. The doors open.

My son, if he doesn't listen to me – like I didn't listen – then he'll end up like me, working long hours for short money for the rest of his life. I want him to do well in education. Be qualified enough to go into something professional. Doesn't have to be anything he doesn't want to do. Some of my mates did really well at school. One of them went into accounting, another did law and they're both now doing something else that's got nothing to do with what they studied. They made a bad choice somewhere. I don't know if it was them or their parents, but they should have studied what they wanted to study; what they enjoyed.

My son, he's only young, but you think about these things. Everyone thinks about their kids and what's best for them. The only thing I can do is do what my dad did for us. I've got to work to make sure they're not going without. Tell them the same things my dad told me: read, educate yourself, don't waste your youth dossing around with your mates because, in the end, you're on your own out there. That's what I did – used to just hang around and do nowt most of the time. Had a laugh, have to admit, but it costs you in the long run. If I'd have studied better who knows? All I can do is try to influence him: 'Look, these are the mistakes I made.' I've just got one but I've got lots of little nephews and nieces and they're like my own, as well. I'm always telling them but who knows if they're listening. Children and the old ones, their *zid*, it's the same: the older you get, the more childish you get.

My dad's still got it in his head that he's gonna go back or we're gonna go back at some stage. When he says that or goes on about the houses he's built in Pakistan, I think, 'Yeah, Dad. Sure – keep dreaming.' The only way I'll ever go back to live for good to Pakistan is if I'm kicked out of this country. Daft as it sounds, it might happen. You never know. Before, that wasn't even on my mind but all this 9/11 has really put pressure on us, not because we're Pakistani, but as Muslims. Government's always questioning everything we do, these days. What goes on in mosques, in homes, in schools – everywhere. It's like us, as Muslims, we're Public Enemy Number One. It gets to you. It's bound to get to you. You try to shrug it off but it keeps coming back at you, keeps getting worse.

One thing that stands in my mind was what happened when them Twin Towers went down. People were really giving it everything about Islam and Muslims as being all crazy terrorists. I was sort of used to that. That was going on from before, in the news and on telly – every time Muslim or Islam was said, it was done in a bad way, a negative spin on it. But then, after this 9/11 happened, I remember there was this big brouhaha: 'How come Muslims aren't apologising for what happened in

America, in New York?' I was shocked by that. Why should I apologise for what someone else did? So what if they did it in the name of Islam? Them Al-Qaeedas, they're the ones that did it, not me, not my neighbour and not any of the people who I know. It's like saying all Christians should apologise because of what Hitler or what's his name – that other guy, in Serbia – did. Hitler was a Christian but no, it's different when it comes to that. You got politicians like Blair and that saying, 'Oh yeah, Muslims are good and peaceful people. Most of them are really sound.' But to me that's patronising and insulting. I don't need anyone to tell me what I am, that my religion is acceptable to them.

There was this Muslim group – Muslim Council or something like that. I remember this, I saw it on the telly and I remember having a right argument about it with one of my brothers. It was a little while after 9/11, and this group, they went and gave a sort of apology. I was sick, me. Why apologise? Why lower yourself? Why not apologise for everything else that's bad and been done by a Muslim? It's like telling the world: 'Us Muslims, we're alright. We won't bomb you or terrorise you or kill you. And even though we got fuck-all to do with 9/11, we're still sorry.' How stupid was that? My brother, though, he thought it was good because it was trying to show the world that we're not all like that, we're not all extreme. But we're not all extreme in the first place, that's what got me. Why should anyone take the blame for what someone else has done? That's wrong. It's double standards. I'll apologise when all Christians start apologising for all the black people that were lynched in America during slavery, or when they

212

apologise for all the people that are still being killed today in Iraq and everywhere else.

I know a few people – probably more than a few people – who were sort of happy about what happened. To them, 9/11 was the same as what goes on in Palestine, Iraq, Chechnya, Kashmir and all those places. You reap what you sow. Everyone knows America's not squeaky clean and some people are probably thinking it serves them right. But me, no, I didn't think that. It wasn't right. Innocent people got killed. No one got Bush or the rest of his cronies. Doesn't matter what religion they are or who they are, but you can't do that to innocent civilians. Someone told me it says in the *Qur'an* that taking the life of one innocent person is like killing the whole of humanity. That says a lot.

A day or two after 7/7 they said it were *aapnay* who did it, from Leeds. I was watching the news. BBC One, this were. Up to then I had a lot of time for BBC news but after that, I thought they're all the same. First they went on about it, that these suicide bombers were home-grown and how bad that is. Fair enough, it is bad – it's a big thing to worry about but there was no real questioning of why these idiots did what they did. They were suicide bombers because they were Muslims and that's all the explanation that you need. Then, same news programme, they went on about how suicide bombers had killed over five hundred people in Israel over the years. Fair enough, that's a lot of people to have killed and it needs saying. But what also needs saying is how many people the Israelis have killed as well. I'm no expert and I don't bet, but if I did, I'd put everything I have on Israelis having killed a lot more than five hundred Palestinians. Never mind Palestinians, I remember a couple of year ago – soldiers killed this English guy, a reporter or a charity worker, he was. He was a civilian, he didn't do nowt – why shoot that poor idiot? What about *those* atrocities? How much time on the news do *they* get? Fifty-odd people died in London because of those bombs; two days later twenty-odd kids – *kids* – were killed in Iraq when some bastard car bombed them. Those kids, they were innocent and they were Muslims so what's that say about the religion of the bombers?

For me, that's what's making things worse – there's no balance, it's all one-sided. Muslims are getting shafted all over the world – Iraq, Afghanistan, Chechnya, Palestine and wherever – but we're painted as the biggest criminals, the real savages, the bad barbarians, too. The killing that Muslims do – which is smaller in number than the killing everyone else does – Russians, Americans, Israelis and that – is like a million times worse.

After the news, I flipped channels and on BBC Three, they were showing Rambo, the first one, *First Blood*, it's called. I've seen it before but I watched it again and there was a bit in it that sort of made me think about what's going on now. There's a bit where a copper says something like, 'Why did God make a guy like Rambo?' and the next thing you know, you hear this voice say, 'God didn't make Rambo, I did.' The guy behind the voice is this colonel in the American Army, Trautman. And that's what we've got now. These people who are happy to blow themselves up and take a few people with them – men, women, kids, old, young, black, white, whatever – that's what they are. They're made by blokes like Trautman. Bin Laden himself is an Arab Rambo, if you think about it, the Americans loved him when he killed the people they didn't like, when them Russians were in Afghanistan. These people, suicide bombers, they're a result of those decisions, those adventures, those little wars and whatever. People don't suddenly decide, 'Oh, I think I'll get on a bus and blow myself up, today.' What's around them, the world they see, hear and feel all around them – that's what turns them. That's their Trautman.

Killing people, civilians, in whatever way, has to be wrong. Myself, I understand why these idiots did what they did but I don't agree with it. I know how they see it. For them, killing ordinary people – believe it or not – is a part of war. Why they do it is because to them it's an eye for an eye, tit for tat. You kill our civilians, we'll kill yours, end of story. It's a simple way of looking at it because by doing that, you're saying you can only fight fire with fire. There has to come a time when you think, 'Hang on a second, nothing's happening here. All that's happening is innocent people – not the ones in power – are getting wasted.'

Even before it happened in London, even them Twin Towers – 9/11 – I didn't agree with it, suicide bombing. But people like me, we can't really understand the conditions in places where there is bad stuff happening. A guy like me, how the hell can he relate to life in Gaza or wherever? That's what surprised me about these lads from Leeds. What was in their heads? What made them do what they did?

I wouldn't call myself religious but I am a Muslim. I just don't practice as much as I should. One day, *inshallah*, I hope to be a better, more practicing Muslim. It's in your heart, you know it makes sense. It's a sort of logical religion, if you think about it. It's got all the answers about how to conduct yourself, how to live your life. That's what people say about Islam – it's more than a religion, it's a way of life.

My wife, she comes from a religious family so she's always been religious. Prays five times a day when she can, makes sure all the kids in the family know what's what, helps them out with their mosque work. They all go to mosque. Monday to Friday, four 'til six. Does them good. They learn about who they are, what they are and it gives them discipline and knowledge. Where else would they learn that? Not in school. Mosques, they're alright now but they could be better. They're miles better than they used to be. I went to mosque but it wasn't that good. It was in a house. We used to have an *Ustaad* and he never charged a penny which is why a lot of people sent their kids there. These days mosques charge a few pounds for a week's worth of teaching which is fair enough. If you want anything of quality, then it costs money. But when I was reading in mosque, it was dangerous. The *Ustaad*, I shouldn't say anything too bad about him, but he could be nasty. Used to have like this thin stick by his side – used to call it his *pehntee*. If you got that on your hand, you knew about it. I had it a few times. Do more than make your eyes water. You'd get it for either not knowing your *sabak* or for arsing about or talking when you were supposed to be reading. They don't do that now. If they do, I don't know about it. None of the kids have complained about it so far.

At first getting married made no difference to me at all. I'd still go out and doss around but then, when she got pregnant, I changed my ways a bit. When he was born, I changed a lot.

Hell of a lot. Still got my old friends but my family and my son comes first now. Before I used to take everyone for granted — even my own parents and relatives. Being a parent myself has opened my eyes. You got to think about everything. Being a parent, it's not that I think it's a bad thing but you can do it badly so easily. So far I don't think I made any mistakes. You have to be more careful with the decisions you make because it's not just you any more who'll pay for the mistake. Like now, my son's schooling is bothering me. Before, I wouldn't have given two shits about schools. But now, every time they publish school league tables in the paper, I'm looking through them. In Bradford, there's hardly any schools that you'd call decent. Across the board, that is — except for like one or two but getting into them is like breaking into a bank. As far as I'm concerned, that's the worst thing about Bradford. The riots and all that is nowt compared to how crap the schools are. I bet there are more teachers who move through Bradford than anywhere else.

For me, Bradford and this area — Manningham — is the zone. You can't beat it. I know I'm only saying that because I live here but that's what it is to me — it's home and it's where my heart is. I know I couldn't live in Pakistan. Couldn't live anywhere else, either. I wouldn't move for anything. I know it's sort of selfish, but I really should be thinking about moving out of the town altogether. I can't see things getting better for my son and for schools, that's the only reason, really. I want him to do well. Even a crap school will do its best but I don't want to take that chance. With me it's too late but my son, he's still got time.

Glossary Of Terms

325 convertible – BMW model/variant.

Aapna – one of us/our own (male).

Aapnay/s – our own people.

Aapnee – one of us/our own (female).

Aapnee zabaan bolo – speak your own language.

Alhamdulilla – 'praise be to Allah'.

Asalamoalaikum-Walaikumsalaam – Muslim greeting and response.

Baycharay – poor/pitiable.

Beenie – traditional Pakistani arm wrestling/arm holding sport.

Biradari – 'brotherhood'. Extended clan/tribal networks and systems of allegiance.

Biradari na bandah – literally translated as 'person of (our) *biradari*'.

Blingers – in this context, street slang for people who are showing off wealth through the wearing of expensive and ostentatious jewellery, clothing and/or other adornments (motor cars can also be 'bling', 'bling-bling' or 'blinging'). *Bling*: the imagined sound of something that 'sparkles'.

BMs – BMW motor cars.

BRI – Bradford Royal Infirmary.

Buddee – old woman.

Buss kar, chup kar. Muree atch see, tharee ami, ala. Buss kar, huhn –

Literally translated as: 'Stop it. Be quiet. She 'll come back, your mum, alright. Stop it, now.'

Calendar News – Yorkshire TV region news programme.

Committee – community/cooperative savings scheme.

Daar – borrowed/loans (money).

Daaree – beard.

Daily Jang – British-based Urdu language newspaper.

Dolee – Pakistani/South Asian wedding carriage/horse.

Five-O – slang for police. Derived from 'Hawaii Five-O'.

Foot patrol – on foot.

Gora – white male.

Goray – white people.

Goree – white female.

Grahn – village.

Gunned – vehicle speed measured by a police officer using a 'speed gun'.

Hijab – head scarf/covering worn by some Muslim females.

'Hood – short for neighbourhood, often mentioned with reference to popular representations of American inner cities.

Imam – various depths of meaning but in this context refers to a religious leader or teacher.

Iman – faith.

Impreza – High performance car manufactured by Subaru Motors.

Insaaneeyat – humanity.

Inshallah – if Allah wills it/Allah willing.

Jilbab – long coat/gown worn by some Muslim females.

Jumma – congregational Friday (midday) prayers.

Kabadi – traditional Pakistani/Indian sport.

Label – designer label.

Lexus – Japanese prestige marque.

Look North – Yorkshire region BBC news programme.

Lulloo – a derogatory term loosely translated as idiot, fool.

M3 – BMW sports/prestige car.

M606 - Industrial/Trading Estate located near the M606 motorway.

Maamoo – maternal uncle.

Madrassah – Islamic religious school/facility; 'supplementary school'.

Mangaythurs – (male) marriage partners from Pakistan.

Manj – ox/buffalo.

Maulvi – Muslim scholar/teacher.

Mawa – maternal uncle.

MC – hip hop term for a rapper (derived from 'Master of Ceremonies').

Mudda – 'mother', usually used within the context of swearing.

Namaz – prayers.

Nangee gayanh, fir utheh ney utheh poacheeh gayanh – literally translated as '(we've) gone through again; again we've reached the same place'.

Naraazgee – not on speaking terms, a falling out.

Nikkah/s – wedding/marriage vows.

Pehntee – cane.

Plates – vehicle registration plates.

Prantay – chapattis cooked with butter/ghee.

Rocks – diamonds (jewellery).

Roll a giro – roll a marijuana/cannabis joint.

Roti – Chapatti.

Sabak – work/lesson.

Shaitan – Satan.

T & A – Telegraph and Argus. Local daily newspaper.

Thaleem – education.

Tthhreeh Pownd – thirty pounds.

Ustaad – teacher.

Walaythee – British.

XR2 – Ford Fiesta 'hot hatchback' variant, popular in the 1980s/90s.

Z3 – BMW variant (2 seater sports).

Zid – stubbornness.

British-Pakistani Men from Bradford:
Linking Narratives to Policy

The formal Research Report made to the Joseph Rowntree Foundation (JRF) is available online as a downloadable pdf file (see: **www.jrf.org.uk/bookshop/**) or as a hard copy format from the JRF directly.

The Joseph Rowntree Foundation

The Joseph Rowntree Foundation has supported the work on which this book is based as part of its programme of research and innovative development projects, which it hopes will be of value to policymakers, practitioners and service users.

The JRF is one of the largest social policy research and development charities in the UK, spending about £7 million a year on programmes of research and development that seeks to better understand the causes of social difficulties and explore ways of overcoming them.

The JRF has decided to broaden its existing knowledge base in the City of Bradford with a 10-year commitment to improving life in Bradford communities. This will be done through ongoing research and development work as well as working in partnership with local people on housing and care projects.